I0113639

Scottish-American Court Records,
1733-1783

Scottish-American COURT RECORDS

1733-1783

David Dobson

CLEARFIELD

Copyright © 1991
Genealogical Publishing Co., Inc.
Baltimore, Maryland
All Rights Reserved.

Library of Congress Catalogue Card Number 91-70282

Reprinted for Clearfield Company by
Genealogical Publishing Company
Baltimore, Maryland
2011

ISBN 978-0-8063-1312-2

Made in the United States of America

Introduction

The political union of Scotland and England in 1707 led to a rapid expansion of Scottish economic links, and subsequent settlement, in the American colonies. By mid-century an influential network of Scottish merchants and planters, connected through blood and business, had been established throughout North America and the West Indies. This network was at its most powerful on the Chesapeake, where in the years prior to the Revolution the tobacco trade was controlled by Glasgow-based merchants and their factors.

Evidence of this economic expansion and subsequent settlement in America exists in a wide range of documentary sources in Scotland, including the records of the Scottish legal system, which have been deposited in the Scottish Record Office in Edinburgh. This volume is based on the minute books of the Court of Session (the highest civil court) and those of the High Court of the Admiralty (which had jurisdiction in all seafaring and maritime cases) for the period 1733–1783. In essence it identifies those people resident in North America who were engaged in litigation in Scotland and whose cases came before the aforementioned courts.

David Dobson

SCOTTISH-AMERICAN COURT RECORDS

ADAIR, JOHN. John Adair, merchant in Antigua, Rev. John Ramsay in Jamaica, Robert Loch in Jamaica, George Murray, merchant in Jamaica, Alexander Baine, merchant in Virginia, & Abraham Soloman, merchant in Jamaica, V. Ebenezer McCulloch & Company, 9 Feb. 1771. (CS16.1.143)

ADAMS, JOHN. John Adams, merchant in Glasgow, V. William MacFarlane, sailor on the St George, re transactions in Jamaica, 29 Oct. 1756. (AC7.48.930)

ADAMSON, ALEXANDER. Alexander Adamson in Jamaica, Lauchlan McQuarrie of Ulva, Samuel Cruickshanks in Jamaica, Richard Beithan, customs controller in the Isle of Man, & Alexander Campbell in Islay then in Jamaica V. Alexander Ross, 29 June 1780. (CS16.1.179)

ADDISON, JOHN. John Addison, music teacher in Jamaica then in Edinburgh, V. John, Lord Oliphant, 21 Nov. 1776. (CS16.1.170)

ADDISON, ROBERT. Robert Addison, goldsmith in Virginia, V. Thomas Irvine, merchant in Gothenburg, Sweden, 1 July 1778. (CS16.1.173)

AINSLIE, THOMAS. Thomas Ainslie, customs controller in Quebec, V. Charles Keir of Overwells, 12 Feb. 1778. (CS16.1.173)

AINSLIE, THOMAS. Thomas Ainslie, customs collector in Quebec, V. William Riddell, 17 Dec. 1782. (CS17.1.1)

AITCHISON, THOMAS. Thomas Aitchison, merchant in Glasgow then in Virginia, V. Andrew Cochrane, merchant in Glasgow, 20 June 1764. (CS16.1.117)

AITCHISON, THOMAS. Thomas Aitchison, merchant in Glasgow then in Virginia, V. Montgomery & Scott, merchants in Glasgow, 5 Dec. 1764. (CS16.1.120)

AITCHISON & RAE. Aitchison & Rae, merchants in Glasgow then in Virginia, V. William Robertson, merchant in Glasgow, 5 July 1764. (CS16.1.117)

1

AITKEN, JOHN. John Aitken, in Sandhills of Kilbarchan,
    Renfrewshire then at Pincader Meeting House,
    Newcastle County, Delaware, V. William Semple, hosier
    in Kilbarchan, & John Semple in Maryland, 14 Dec. 1774.
                                              (CS16.1.161)

AITKEN, MATTHEW.   Matthew Aitken in Maryland V. Margaret
    Barr in Yeatston, widow of Alexander Alexander, etc.,
    2 Dec. 1777.   (CS16.1.151)

AITKEN, MATTHEW.   Matthew Aitken in America, son of James
    Aitken in Sandholes, V. William Barr in Paisley,
    23 Jan. 1783.   (CS17.1.2)

ALEXANDER, ALEXANDER JOHN.   Alexander John Alexander,
    planter & merchant in the Grenades, V. Alexander
    Crichton, coachmaker in Canongate, 7 Feb. 1778.
                                              (CS16.1.173)

ALEXANDER OF NEWTON, CLAUD.   Claud Alexander of Newton V.
    James Johnston & John Hood, merchants in Glasgow then
    in Virginia, re shipment on the Joanna of Glasgow to
    the James River, Virginia, 8 July 1760.   (AC7.50)

ALEXANDER, JOHN.   John Alexander, merchant in Grenada, &
    William Alexander, merchant in Edinburgh, V. Isobel
    Ross, 26 Nov. 1777.   (CS16.1.171)

ALEXANDER, WILLIAM.   William Alexander & .... Mitchell,
    merchants in Antigua, V. Samuel Crawford & Company,
    merchants in Glasgow, 17 Feb. 1773.   (CS16.1.154)

ALEXANDER & MITCHELL.   Alexander & Mitchell, merchants in
    Antigua, V. William Laing, merchant in Glasgow,
    9 DEc. 1778.   (CS16.1.174)

ALISON, JOHN.   John Alison, merchant in Glasgow then in
    Virginia, V. John Steven, merchant in Glasgow,
    22 June 1748.   (CS16.1.80)

ALISON, JOHN.   John Alison, merchant in Glasgow then in
    Virginia, V. Elizabeth Warden, widow of Arthur Tran,
    merchant in Glasgow, 22 June 1748.   (CS16.1.80)

ALISON, WILLIAM.   William Alison, physician in Edinburgh
    then in Virginia, & George Begbie, cowfeeder in Canon-
    gate, V. Robert Sym, 9 Feb. 1748.   (CS16.1.80)

                              2

ALISON, WILLIAM.   Dr William Alison, surgeon in Virginia, V.
Fxancis Crawford, dean of the wrights in Glasgow,
25 Feb. 1749.   (CS16.1.81)

ALLAN, JAMES.   James Allan, cabinetmaker & joiner in
Fredericksburg, Spotsylvania County, Virginia, V.
Christian Allan in Hamilton, 7 Dec. 1763.   (CS16.1.117)

ALLAN, JAMES.   James Allan & John Allan in Kingston, Jamaica,
V. Andrew Jack, merchant in Glasgow, 9 July 1783.
                                                 (CS17.1.2)

ALLAN, RICHARD.   Richard Allan, student of physics in
Edinburgh then in North America, V. Mary Nasmyth, wife of
James Latto farmer in Geilsyards, 3 Dec. 1778.
                                                 (CS16.1.174)

ALLASON, JOHN.   John Allason in Virginia, eldest son of John
Allason in Glasgow, V. John Buchanan, factor to Lord
Cathcart, 16 Dec. 1772.   (CS16.1.151)

ALLASON, JOHN.   John Allason in Virginia, eldest son of John
Allason, butcher in Glasgow, V. Robert Stevenson in Tit-
wood, 16 Dec. 1772.   (CS16.1.151)

ALLASON, JOHN.   John Allason in Virginia, eldest son of John
Allason, butcher in Glasgow, V. John McAdam of Craigin-
gella, 1 Dec. 1773.   (CS16.1.157)

ALLASON, JOHN.   John Allason in Virginia, eldest son of John
Allason, butcher in Glasgow, V. William McIlwraith of
Kirkland, 19 Jan. 1774.   (CS16.1.157)

ALLASON, JOHN.   John Allason, merchant in St Kitts, Alexander
Graham, merchant in Glasgow, & William Hodgzart, merchant
in New York, V. Alston, Carmalt & Company, merchants in
Greenock, 17 July 1782.   (CS17.1.1)

ALSTON, GEORGE.   George Alston & William Littlejohn, merchants
in North Carolina, V. John Alston jr, merchant in
Glasgow, 22 Jan. 1783.   (CS17.1.2)

AMOS, JOHN.   John Amos, merchant in London then in North
America, V. William Ballantyne, merchant in London, &
Matthew Irving, merchant in Langholm, 21 June 1775.
                                                 (CS16.1.165)

3

ANDERSON, ANDREW. Andrew Anderson, merchant in Glasgow
    then in Virginia, V. Arthur Nasmith in Hamilton,
    18 June 1747.   (CS16.1.79)

ANDERSON, WILLIAM. William Anderson, merchant in Virginia,
    & Margaret Brown, widow of Andrew Ross, Professor of
    Humanity at Glasgow University, V. John Campbell of
    Whitehaugh, merchant in Ayr, 27 Feb. 1750. (CS16.1.84)

ANDERSON, WILLIAM. William Anderson, merchant in Jamaica, V.
    the trustees of James Anderson, merchant in Glasgow,
    25 Jan. 1774.   (CS16.1.157)

ANNANDALE, WILLIAM. William Annandale, tailor in King George
    County, Rappahannock, Virginia, V. William McIntosh,
    writer in Edinburgh, 12 June 1744.   (CS16.1.73)

ANNANDALE, WILLIAM. William Annandale, tailor in Virginia,
    & John Anderson, writer in Edinburgh, V. Peter Brown,
    wigmaker in Edinburgh, Nov. 1749.   (CS16.1.81)

ARTHUR, JAMES. James Arthur, merchant on the James River,
    Virginia, V. Hugh Stewart, merchant in Glasgow,
    31 July 1751.   (CS16.1.85)

AULD, ROBERT. Robert Auld, master of the **Pelican of Salt-
    coats**, V. James Montier, Peter Montgomery, William
    Gordon & Henry McCaull, merchants in Glasgow, re a
    voyage to Barbados & Antigua, 22 Feb. 1734. (AC7.40.166)

AVEN, ARCHIBALD. Rev. Archibald Aven, London then in
    Norfolk, Virginia, V. Alexander Aven, merchant in
    Banff, 23 Feb. 1774.   (CS16.1.157)

BAILLIE, BRIDGET. Bridget Baillie, widow of James Donaldson,
    merchant in Maryland, & their son James Donaldson V.
    William Donaldson of Murroch, 27 Jan. 1748. (CS16.1.80)

BAILLIE, THOMAS. Thomas Baillie in Charleston, South
    Carolina, V. John Watson, merchant in South Carolina,
    22 Nov. 1743.   (CS16.1.73)

BAILLI, THOMAS. Thomas Baillie, merchant in Charleston, South
    Carolina, V. Margaret & Helen Baillie, daughters of Hugh
    Baillie, customs collector in Orkney, 20 Dec. 1743.
                                                    (CS16.1.73)

4

BAIN, ROBERT.   Robert Bain, merchant in Richmond, Virginia,
    & Robert Watson, lately a medical student in Edinburgh,
    V. David Ross, trustee of McPherson & Grant, merchants
    in Edinburgh, 8 Aug. 1775.   (CS16.1.165)

BAIRD, JAMES.   James Baird, shipmaster in Glasgow then a
    merchant in Virginia, V. David Dalrymple & Company,
    merchants in Glasgow, 5 Dec. 1764.   (CS16.1.120)

BALLANTYNE, JOHN.   John Ballantyne, Ebenezer McHarg &
    Anthony McKitterick, merchants in Virginia, V. James
    Johnston & Company, merchants in Glasgow, 2 Feb. 1763.
                                                  (CS16.1.115)

BANNATYNE.   Bannatyne, McHarg & McKitterick, merchants in
    Virginia, V. Andrew Cochran, John Bowman & Walter
    Monteith, merchants in Glasgow, 3 July 1765.(CS16.1.122)

BANNATYNE, JAMES.   James Bannatyne, writer in Edinburgh then
    in Jamaica, V. William Tytler, 16 July 1783. (CS17.1.2)

BARCLAY, GILBERT.   Gilbert Barclay, merchant in Boston, &
    James Veitch, surgeon on the King George packet boat at
    Falmouth, V. Donald Edie, shipmaster in Leith, 9 Feb. 1763.
                                                  (CS16.1.115)

BEAN, SAMUEL.   Samuel Bean, merchant in Jamaica then in
    London, V. Newton, Gordon & Johnston, merchants in
    Madeira, 8 Mar. 1781.   (CS16.1.183)

BEATTIE, WILLIAM.   William Beattie, merchant in Virginia then
    in Dumfries, V. Reid & Steuart, merchants in London,
    3 Nov. 1749.   (CS16.1.81)

BENNET, MAXWELL.   Maxwell Bennet, writer in Edinburgh then
    in Jamaica, Lieutenant Hamilton of the 37th Regiment in
    America, & Balfour Stewart, collector of taxes in Wick,
    Caithness, V. trustees of Charles Butter, merchant in
    Edinburgh, 11 Mar. 1780.   (CS16.1.179)

BERTRAM, ALEXANDER.   Alexander Bertram, eldest son of George
    Bertram blacksmith in Biggar, merchant in Philadelphia,
    V. James Wilson, tenant farmer in Goatfoot of Skirling,
    4 July 1772.   (CS16.1.151)

BETHUNE, WILLIAM.   William Bethune, merchant in Portree then
    in America, V. Lauchlane McKinnon of Corriechattan, etc,
    19 Dec. 1771.   (CS16.1.148)

5

BLACK, DAVID.   David Black in Boston, William Jamieson,
     merchant in Edinburgh then in Charleston, David Gibson
     at Montego Bay, Jamaica, & John Allan, school-doctor in
     Kirkcaldy then in Nevis, V. John Rintoul & Company,
     merchants in Kirkcaldy, 9 July 1783.   (CS17.1.2)

BLAIR, ARCHIBALD.   Archibald & John Blair, sons of James
     Blair merchant in Virginia, V. John Blair, merchant in
     Edinburgh, 10 Feb. 1773.   (CS16.1.154)

BLAIR, ARCHIBALD.   Archibald & John Blair, sons of James
     Blair merchant in Virginia, V. Alexander Clapperton,
     writer in Edinburgh, 27 Jan. 1774.   (CS16.1.157)

BLAIR, JOHN.   John Blair, merchant in Williamsburg, Virginia,
     eldest son of Peter Blair, skinner in Edinburgh, V. *
     Archibald Blair, writer in Edinburgh, 23 Dec. 1746.
                                                 (CS16.1.79)

BLAW, JAMES.   James Blaw, surgeon in Jamaica, James Blaw,
     merchant in Kirkwall, and his wife Barbara Donaldson, &
     Gilbert Mason, merchant in Edinburgh, V. James Blaw,
     merchant in Kirkwall, 28 July 1779.   (CS16.1.177)

BOG, THOMAS.   Thomas Bog, merchant in North Carolina, V.
     Archibald Iver, shipmaster in Greenock, and his wife
     Christian Iver, 2 Mar. 1774.   (CS16.1.157)

BORLAND, FRANCIS.   Francis Borland, merchant in New England,
     Paul Hamilton in Edisto Island, South Carolina, John
     Cumming, merchant in Glasgow, eldest son of Matthew
     Cumming & Margaret Kincaid, 8 Feb. 1743.   (CS16.1.72)

BORELAND, ROBERT.   Robert Boreland, surgeon in Jamaica, V.
     Patrick Grieve of Law, 8 Aug. 1772.   (CS16.1.151)

BORTHWICK, JOHN.   John Borthwick, merchant in Edinburgh then
     in North America, V. Peter Ramsay, magistrate of Pitten-
     weem, 22 June 1770.   (CS16.1.141)

BORTHWICK, JOHN.   John Borthwick, merchant in Edinburgh then
     in America, V. Agnes, Mary & Margaret Boyack, 25 Feb. 1772.
                                                 (CS16.1.148)

BOSWELL, DAVID.   David Boswell in Jamaica, son of David
     Boswell, V. William Campbell, 8 July 1778. (CS16.1.173)

BOYD, JAMES.   James Boyd, son of William Boyd of Trochrig,
    in America, V. Archibald Crawford of Ardmillan,
    13 Dec. 1781.   (CS16.1.184)

BOYD, JOHN.   John Boyd, writer in Irvine then a merchant in
    New York, V. John & Hugh Parker, merchants in
    Kilmarnock, 6 Aug. 1778.   (CS16.1.174)

BOYD, MARY JANET.   Mary Janet Boyd, in Charleston South
    Carolina, daughter of Robert Boyd, merchant in South
    Carolina, V. William, Mary & Christian Kelly, children
    of George Kelly, merchant in Dunbar, 9 July 1773.
                                               (CS16.1.154)

BOYD, MARY.   Mary Boyd, daughter of Robert Boyd, merchant in
    Charleston, South Carolina, & Ann Walker, V. Charles &
    Robert Falls, merchants in Dunbar, 6 Aug. 1768.
                                               (CS16.1.133)

BOYD, ROBERT.   Robert Boyd, merchant in Charleston, South
    Carolina, V. Charles & Robert Falls, merchants in
    Dunbar, 18 Feb. 1767.   (CS16.1.126)

BOYD, ROBERT.   Robert Boyd, merchant in Charleston, South
    Carolina, & William Murray, merchant in Edinburgh, V.
    David Edie, shipmaster, & David Loch, merchant in Leith,
    14 Aug. 1767.   (AC7.52)

BOYD, SPENCER.   Spencer Boyd, eldest son of James Boyd,
    physician at West Point, York River, Virginia, & John
    Brown, merchant in Glasgow, V. Ann Boyd, daughter of
    Robert Boyd of Penkill, wife of William Boyd of Troch-
    rigg, and the said William Boyd, 17 Feb. 1774.
                                               (CS16.1.157)

BOYLE, JAMES LAWRENCE.   James Lawrence Boyle, son of John
    Boyle, merchant in St Croix, V. Katherine & Margaret
    Boyle, nieces of Dr James Stewart of Christwell,
    22 Jan. 1783.   (CS17.1.2)

BOYLE, JAMES.   James Boyle, eldest son of John Boyle,
    surgeon in St Eustatia, & Agnes Boyle, wife of John Key,
    tailor in St Eustatia, V. David Stewart, 4 July 1781.
                                               (CS16.1.183)

BOYLE, JAMES LAWRENCE.   James Lawrence Boyle, son of John
    Boyle, merchant in St Croix, V. Katherine Boyle, wife of
    Patrick Colquhoun, brewer in Crawfordykes, 11 Mar. 1778.
                                               (CS16.1.173)

BOYLE, JAMES LAWRENCE. James Lawrence Boyle, son of John
Boyle, merchant in St Croix, V. James Brisbane, son of
Matthew Brisbane, wright in Greenock, & his wife
Margaret Boyle, Katherine Boyle, widow of Patrick
Colquhoun, brewer in Crawfordykes, & Agnes Boyle, widow
of John Kay, tailor in St Eustatia, 24 Jan. 1782.
(CS17.1.1)

BREADIE, ROBERT. Robert Breadie, merchant in Perth then in
South Carolina, & William Breadie, merchant in Perth,
heir of James Breadie, merchant in Perth, V. John
Wedderspoon, merchant in Perth, 20 June 1781.(CS16.1.183)

BREADIE, ROBERT. Robert Breadie, merchant in Perth then in
South Carolina, V. Thomas Mitchell, writer in Perth,
23 Nov. 1781. (CS16.1.184)

BRISBANE, EDWARD. Edward Brisbane in North America, son of
Patrick Brisbane in Glasgow, & John Simpson in America,
son of Matthew Simpson in Glasgow, etc. V. Archibald
Roberton of Bedlay, 10 July 1778. (CS16.1.173)

BROWN, GEORGE. George Brown, merchant in Norfolk, Virginia,
V. John Greenlees & Thomas Hardie, merchants in Norfolk,
Virginia, 11 Mar. 1766. (CS16.1.125)

BROWN, GRIERSON & COMPANY. Brown, Grierson & Company,
merchants in Norfolk, Virginia, V. Alexander Wilson &
Son, typemakers in Glasgow, 7 Feb. 1776. (CS16.1.168)

BROWN, GUSTAVUS. Gustavus Brown in Maryland V. Robert
Trotter of Mainside, 14 Dec. 1741. (CS16.1.69)

BROWN, THOMAS. Thomas Brown in Virginia then in Fenwick &
James Boyd of Penkill V. James Brown, merchant in
Glasgow, 11 Dec. 1782. (CS17.1.1)

BROWN, THOMAS. Thomas Brown, merchant in King & Queen County,
Virginia, then in Fenwick, Ayrshire, V. James Boyd in
King & Queen County, Virginia, 5 Mar. 1783. (CS17.1.2)

BROWN, WILLIAM. William Brown in Jamaica, eldest son of
Alexander Brown, writer in Airdrie, V. John Aitchison,
22 July 1773. (CS16.1.154)

BROWN, ... Rev. Brown, Church of England clergyman in
Maryland or Virginia, & Isabel, widow of Rev. Patrick
Adair, in Carrickfergus, etc. V. Charles Dalrymple of
Orangefield, 21 July 1767.   (CS16.1.130)

BRUCE, JAMES.   Edward Bruce, James Bruce in Jamaica, Betty
Pomeroy Bruce, wife of Robert McGhie in Jamaica, V.
Archibald Kent, 28 Jan. 1783.   (CS17.1.2)

BRUCE, JAMES.   James Bruce in Jamaica, etc. V. James Torry,
3 Feb. 1773.   (CS16.1.154)

BRYCE, ALEXANDER.   Alexander Bryce in Grenada, eldest son of
Nicol Bryce, merchant in Stirling, V. William Wright,
merchant in Stirling, 18 Mar. 1779.   (CS16.1.175)

BRYCE, WILLIAM.   William Bryce, merchant in Glasgow, V.
Ninian Bryce, shipmaster in Glasgow, re a voyage to
New England, 6 Jan. 1738.   (AC7.43.4)

BUCHANAN, ANDREW.   Andrew Buchanan, merchant in Virginia,
eldest son of George Buchanan, merchant in Glasgow, etc.
V. James Buchanan of Drumpelier, 21 Dec. 1776.
                                                    (CS16.1.170)

BUCHANAN, ARCHIBALD.   Archibald Buchanan of Drumhead,
merchant in Virginia, eldest son of Archibald Buchanan
of Drumhead, tide-surveyor in Greenock, V. Robert
Muschet of Green, 4 June 1751.   (CS16.1.85)

BUCHANAN, ARCHIBALD.   Archibald Buchanan of Drumhead,
merchant in Norfolk, Virginia, son of Archibald
Buchanan, V. Gilbert, James, John, Dorothy, Janet, Jean,
Margaret, & Rebecca Buchanan, younger children of
Archibald Buchanan of Drumhead, & Robert Shewman, ship-
master in Greenock, husband of said Dorothy, 14 Feb. 1750.
                                                    (CS16.1.84)

BUCHANAN, ARCHIBALD.   Archibald Buchanan of Drumhead,
merchant in Virginia, V. Isabel Buchanan & her husband
William Crawford, watchmaker in Glasgow, 31 July 1751.
                                                    (CS16.1.85)

BUCHANAN, GEORGE.   George Buchanan, merchant in Glasgow then
in Virginia, Neil Buchanan, Duncan Rose, & Robert Baillie,
merchants in Glasgow, Daniel McLean, merchant in Glasgow
then in America, V. William Wilson, 9 JUly 1773.
(CS16.1.154)

BUCHANAN, NEIL.   Neil Buchanan, merchant in Virginia,
William Jamieson, merchant in Virginia, & John Fisher,
merchant in Virginia, V. John Brown, mason in Dunbarton,
15 July 1778.   (CS16.1.173)

BUCHANAN, WILLIAM.   William Buchanan in America, eldest son
of Alexander Buchanan of Auchenmar, V. William Campbell
of Glensalloch, 4 Dec. 1771.   (CS16.1.146)

BUNTEIN, THOMAS.   Thomas Buntein in Port Royal, Jamaica, son
of Robert Buntein of Mildowan, etc. V. William Loch,
writer in Edinburgh, 28 June 1754.   (CS16.1.92)

BURD, JAMES.   James Burd, Colonel of the Provincial Regiment
of Pennsylvania, & John Hawthorn of Auries, V. The Bank
of Scotland, 8 Aug. 1775.   (CS16.1.165)

BURD, JAMES.   Lieutenant Colonel James Burd, Provincial
Service in America, V. Margaret & Elizabeth Burd,
daughters of Edward Burd of Ormiston, 4 Mar. 1780.
(CS16.1.179)

BURKE, TOBIAS.   Tobias Burke, blockmaker in Greenock then
in Jamaica, & John Mikle, surgeon in Jamaica, V. John
Smyth, shipmaster in Newton-on-Ayr, 11 Feb. 1781.
(CS16.1.183)

BURN, FINLEY.   Finley Burn, from Glasgow, an officer in a
Provincial Regiment in America, John Lyle, merchant in
Montreal, William Duncan, merchant in Glasgow then in
Virginia, Robert Spence, merchant in New York, & William
Shaw, bookseller in America, V. John Gibson, merchant in
Glasgow, 7 Aug. 1781.   (CS16.1.184)

BURN, JAMES.   James Burn, son of John Burn, in Charleston,
South Carolina, V. William Walker, writer in Edinburgh,
18 Jan. 1775.   (CS16.1.161)

BURN, MARY. Mary Burn, widow of Dr Charles Brown, physician
    in Williamsburg, Virginia, & his daughter Mary Brown, V.
    Alexander Inglis or Hamilton of Murdiestower, John Burn
    of Middlemiln, landwaiter in Alloa, & John Nisbet, writer
    in Edinburgh, 30 July 1741.   (CS16.1.70)

BURTON, WILLIAM. William Burton on the James River, Virginia,
    son of William Burton, landwaiter in Port Glasgow, V.
    Ebenezer Munro, merchant in Glasgow, 28 Jan. 1756.
                                           (CS16.1.95)

BURTON, WILLIAM. William Burton, merchant in Virginia, V.
    James Weir, shipmaster in Port Glasgow, 14 Jan. 1756.
                                           (CS16.1.85)

CAMERON, RICHARD. Richard Cameron, merchant in Glasgow then
    in America, eldest son of John Cameron of Carntyne, V.
    James Berrie, merchant in Glasgow, 11 Mar. 1780.
                                           (CS16.1.179)

CAMPBELL, ALEXANDER. Alexander Campbell, surveyor in Jamaica
    now in Ballole, Islay, V. John Campbell, tacksman of
    Duntoskine, 29 Jan. 1772.   (CS16.1.148)

CAMPBELL, ALEXANDER. Alexander Campbell in Ballole then in
    America, etc. V. Alexander Ross, 5 July 1780.(CS16.1.179)

CAMPBELL, ALEXANDER. Alexander Campbell at Green River,
    Jamaica, etc. V. Alexander Ross, 5 July 1780.(CS16.1.179)

CAMPBELL, ALEXANDER. Alexander Campbell, merchant in Jamaica,
    V. Alexander Campbell, merchant in Glasgow, 9 Dec. 1780.
                                           (CS16.1.181)

CAMPBELL, ANGUS. Angus Campbell in Jura then in Carolina,
    & Charles McArthur in Jamaica, V. Alexander Campbell,
    merchant in Glasgow, 26 July 1780.   (CS16.1.181)

CAMPBELL, ARCHIBALD. Rev. Archibald Campbell in America V.
    Alexander McCallum of Glennan, 9 Mar. 1762. (CS16.1.114)

CAMPBELL, ARCHIBALD. Rev. Archibald Campbell in America,
    brother of Robert Campbell of Kirnan, Marjory Kennell,
    wife of John Black, shoemaker in Edinburgh, V. Duncan
    Campbell of Kirnan, 20 July 1769.   (CS16.1.138)

11

CAMPBELL, ARCHIBALD.   Archibald Campbell, cooper in Greenock
   then in Virginia, V. Mary Campbell, widow of John Paton
   writer in Greenock, and their children William, Lilly &
   Anne, 18 July 1770.   (CS16.1.141)

CAMPBELL, CHARLES.   Charles Campbell, merchant in Virginia
   then in Ayr, V. John Fraser, shipscarpenter in Ayr,
   30 July 1756.   (CS16.1.99)

CAMPBELL, COLIN.   Colin Campbell, mason in Jamaica, Rev.
   Patrick Campbell in Inveraray, etc. V. Hugh Hamilton,
   merchant in Edinburgh, 2 Dec. 1772.   (CS16.1.151)

CAMPBELL, COLIN.   Colin Campbell in America, Archibald
   Campbell in America, Duncan Campbell in Jamaica, William
   Campbell in Jamaica, all sons of William Campbell of
   Glenfalloch, & Captain Robert Campbell in Jamaica and his
   sons James & John Campbell in America, V. John Menzies of
   Culdares, 16 Jan. 1783.   (CS17.1.2)

CAMPBELL, DANIEL.   Daniel Campbell in Jamaica, son of
   Alexander Campbell of Ballochyle, Argyll, V, George
   Scott, merchant in Greenock, 16 June 1773. (CS16.1.154)

CAMPBELL, DONALD.   Donald Campbell in Jamaica, James
   McFarlane in Jamaica, etc. V. Alexander Campbell, merchant
   in Glasgow, 19 July 1780.   (CS16.1.179)

CAMPBELL, DOUGAL.   Dougal Campbell of Laggan, merchant in
   Campbelltown then in North America, V. John Campbell,
   merchant in Campbelltown, 6 Feb. 1777.   (CS16.1.170)

CAMPBELL, DUNCAN.   Duncan Campbell in Kingston, Jamaica, V.
   James Campbell, merchant in Kingston, Jamaica, then in
   Crieff, 27 June 1770.   (CS16.1.141)

CAMPBELL, DUNCAN.   Duncan Campbell, merchant in Kingston,
   Jamaica, V. Alexander Abercrombie, 3 Feb. 1774.
                                                   (CS16.1.84)

CAMPBELL, GILBERT.   Gilbert Campbell, customs controller on
   the Potomac River, Virginia, etc. V. George Veitch,
   merchant in Edinburgh, 21 Dec. 1768.   (CS16.1.134)

CAMPBELL, JAMES.   James Campbell in Crieff then in Tobago,
   V. Duncan Ochiltree of Lindsaig, merchant in Inveraray,
   4 Dec. 1776.   (CS16.1.170)

12

CAMPBELL, JOHN. John Campbell, merchant in St Croix then
    in Greenock, V. Duncan Bruce in Rothesay, 20 Nov. 1776.
                                              (CS16.1.170)

CAMPBELL, JOHN. John Campbell, merchant in Greenock then in
    America, Colin Campbell, merchant in Glasgow then in
    America, V. John Laird & Company in Greenock, 9 July 1783.
                                              (CS17.1.2)

CAMPBELL, JOHN. John Campbell, tailor in New York, son of
    John Campbell in Newcampbellton, V. William Smith,
    merchant in Edinburgh, 17 Dec. 1766.   (CS16.1.126)

CAMPBELL, JOHN. John Campbell in London then in America, &
    Thomas Storrie in London, V. Andrew Thomson of Faskine,
    merchant in Glasgow, 28 June 1768.   (CS16.1.133)

CAMPBELL, MAGDALENE. Magdalene, Jean and Janet Campbell,
    daughters of James Campbell of Burnbank and Margaret
    Cathcart, Dr John Taylor of Pitcairly, husband of the
    said Jean, & ..... Clitheroe, merchant in Carolina,
    husband of the said Magdalene, V. Elizabeth and Jean
    Campbell, daughters of Archibald Campbell, eldest son
    of Colonel James Campbell of Burnbank, 4 July 1750.
                                              (CS16.1.84)

CAMPBELL, MUNGO. Mungo Campbell in the West Indies then in
    Edinburgh, V. George Ferguson, advocate, 15 Nov. 1780.
                                              (CS16.1.181)

CAMPBELL, NEILL. Neill Campbell, shipmaster in Port Glasgow,
    V. Charles Wrightman & Archibald Smith, merchants in
    Tobago, 28 Jan. 1780.   (AC7.57)

CAMPBELL, WILLIAM. William Campbell, merchant in Smith-
    hills of Paisley then in America, V. Robert Brodie,
    merchant in Paisley, 22 Nov. 1780.   (CS16.1.181)

CAMPBELL, WILLIAM. Captain William Campbell in Rhode
    Island, son of George Campbell of Carsegownie and Grizel
    Ogilvy, V. Margaret and Isabel Ogilvy, daughters of
    John Ogilvy of Pitmuies, 6 Aug. 1755.   (CS16.1.95)

CAMPBELL, WILLIAM. Captain William Campbell, shipmaster in
    Rhode Island, & Alexander Watson of Turin, V. James
    Dickson, merchant in Montrose, 8 Aug. 1759. (CS16.1.105)

                        13

CAMPBELL, BLANE & COMPANY.   Campbell, Blane & Company,
    merchants in Grenada, V. Alexander Spalding of Holm,
    3 Dec. 1776.   (CS16.1.170)

CAMPBELL, BLANE & COMPANY.   Campbell, Blane & Company,
    merchants in Grenada, V. George and James McLellan,
    sons of Robert McLellan of Barscob, 22 Jan. 1782.
                                                    (CS16.1.185)

CAMPBELL, BLANE & COMPANY.   Campbell, Blane & Company,
    merchants in St George, Grenada, V. Barbara McLellan,
    6 July 1782.   (CS17.1.1)

CARRUTHERS, ROBERT.   Robert Carruthers, & James Carruthers
    in North Carolina, V. Robert Carruthers, surgeon in
    Wareham, Dorset, 21 Feb. 1781.   (CS16.1.183)

CHALMERS, DONALD.   Donald Chalmers, merchant in Virginia,
    James Chalmers, merchant in Jamaica, Ronald Chalmers,
    farmer in Dilduff, all brothers of John Chalmers,
    merchant in Glasgow, V. Stark, Crosse & Company,
    merchants in Glasgow, 6 Dec. 1765.   (CS16.1.125)

CHALMERS, RONALD.   Ronald Chalmers in Grasford, Carolina,
    V. James Gibson, vintner in Ayr, 9 Jan. 1761,(CS16.1.107)

CHAPMAN, DANIEL.   Daniel Chapman, merchant in Edinburgh then
    in America, etc. V. Mungo Carrick, hosier in Edinburgh,
    27 Jan. 1773.   (CS16.1.154)

CHISHOLM, WILLIAM.   William Chisholm in Jamaica then in
    London V. Robert Napier in Jamaica then in Glasgow,
    11 Aug. 1781.   (CS16.1.184)

CHRISTIE, ADAM.   Adam Christie jr, merchant in Pensacola,
    Alexander & Mitchell, merchants in Antigua, William
    McCaa, merchant in Virginia, John Parker jr, merchant
    in Kingston, Jamaica, John Crichton, mate of the
    Dolphin of Port Glasgow, & John Cramond, merchant in
    Norfolk, Virginia, V. Patrick Telfer, merchant in
    Glasgow, 25 Feb. 1778.   (CS16.1.173)

CHRISTIE, ROBERT.   Robert Christie, merchant in Glasgow then
    in America, V. James Hall & Company, merchants in
    Glasgow, 23 Nov. 1774.   (CS16.1.161)

CLARK, ALEXANDER. Alexander Clark, brother of Daniel
Clark, merchant in Augusta, South Carolina (sic), V.
Margaret Clark, wife of David Fraser, tenant in
Flemington, 15 July 1760. (CS16.1.107)

CLARK, GEORGE. George Clark, former Barrackmaster General
in America, V. Archibald Murray, merchant in Peebles,
27 July 1781. (CS16.1.184)

CLARK, JAMES. James Clark, shoemaker in Edinburgh, V.
James Penman, merchant in St Augustine, Florida,
27 Aug. 1788. (AC7.59)

CLARK, MARGARET. Margaret Clark, niece of Daniel Clark,
merchant in Augusta, South Carolina (sic), and her
husband David Fraser, V. Duncan Clark, merchant in
Inverness, son of Duncan Clark, tobacconist in
Inverness, 29 Jan. 1766. (CS16.1.125)

CLARK, THOMAS. Dr Thomas Clark in Jamaica V. Hugh Corrie,
17 Feb. 1781. (CS16.1.183)

CLARK, ... Clark, wright in Edinburgh then in
America, his wife Jean Campbell, & Lieutenant Robert
Ferguson of the 77th Regiment V. Elizabeth Stewart of
Glenbucket and her husband David Stewart, 15 Feb. 1780.
(CS16.1.179)

CLARKSON, THOMAS. Thomas Clarkson, merchant in Glasgow then
in Barbados, V. Hugh Wyllie, merchant in Glasgow, 3 July
1765. (CS16.1.122)

CLERK, JONATHAN. Jonathan Clerk and John Gutteridge,
merchants in Boston, V. Alexander Thomson, shipmaster
in Leith, re the voyage of the John of Portsmouth, New
Hampshire, from Boston to Leith, 23 Jan. 1739.
(AC7.44.185)

COCHRAN, DAVID. David Cochran, merchant in Virginia,
Thomas Hill, merchant in Glasgow, Stewart McVey and
Thomas Hill in St Kitts, Stewart & George McVey in
St Kitts, Hugh Ross in Montserrat, James MacMillan in
Virginia, Samuel McNeill in St Kitts, Alexander Stewart
in Virginia, Samuel & Hugh McNeill in St Kitts, Robert
Bryce in St Kitts, Adam Stewart in Virginia, Alexander
Cunningham in Virginia, Williamson Grieve & McNeill in
St Kitts, & David Walker in Virginia, V. Greenshields &
Wardrope, merchants in Glasgow, 9 July 1766.(CS16.1.125)

15

COCHRAN, RICHARD. Richard Cochran in New Jersey then in
Glasgow, William Cochran of Kirkfield, & George
Cochran, surgeon in Glasgow, V. Robert McNair, merchant
in Glasgow, 13 Feb. 1780. (CS16.1.181)

COCHRAN, WILLIAM. William Cochran in New Jersey then in
Glasgow V. Thomas McNair, 4 Aug. 1781. (CS16.1.184)

COCHRAN, WILLIAM. William Cochran of Kirkfield, Richard
Cochran in New Jersey then in Glasgow, George
Cochran, surgeon in Glasgow, V. Robert McNair, merchant
in Glasgow, 24 Jan. 1782. (CS17.1.1)

COLE, MARGARET. Margaret Cole, daughter of George Cole in
Jamaica then in Falkland, V. Robert Pringle of Clifton,
21 Jan. 1774. (CS16.1.154)

COLQUHOUN, WALTER. Walter Colquhoun, merchant in Virginia
then in Jamaica, and his mother Margaret Williamson or
Colquhoun, V. Rev. John McAulay in Cardross, 22 Jan.
1783. (CS17.1.2)

COOK, JOHN. John Cook, merchant in Tobago, V. John Douglas,
hatmaker in Edinburgh, 4 Dec. 1782. (CS17.1.1)

COPLAND, WILLIAM. William Copland, butcher in Lockerbie
then in America, V. Sir William Maxwell of Springkell,
2 July 1783. (CS17.1.2)

CORRIE, ARCHIBALD. Archibald Corrie, merchant in Bath and
Edenton, North Carolina, eldest son of James Corrie of
Spedden, Provost of Dumfries, V. Sir Robert Lawrie of
Maxwelltown, 17 Nov. 1770. (CS16.1.143)

CORRIE, JOHN. John Corrie in Providence, Rhode Island,
factor for Walter Corrie in Providence, V. Thomas
Leslie, writer in Linlithgow, 24 Dec. 1740. (CS16.1.69)

CORRIE, JOSEPH. Joseph Corrie in Dominica V. Hugh Corrie,
factor for Alexander Johnston, Hugh Lawson & Company,
bankers in Dumfries, 4 July 1782. (CS17.1.1)

COULTER, JAMES. James Coulter, merchant in Glasgow, V.
Robert and James McNair, merchants in Glasgow, re the
voyage of the _Jean_ to Virginia & Barbados, 19 Mar. 1755.
(AC7.47.32)

CRAIG, JOHN.   John Craig, mariner in Glasgow then in
     Virginia, John Hamilton, physician in Maryland, &
     William Maitland, surgeon, etc. V. Alexander
     Stevenson, commissary clerk in Glasgow, 9 July 1762.
                                              (CS16.1.114)

CRAIGDALLIE, JANET.   Janet Craigdallie, daughter of Hugh
     Craigdallie, surgeon in Princess Anne County,
     Virginia, eldest son of Gilbert Craigdallie, glover
     in Perth, V. Thomas Anderson, merchant in Perth, &
     Lawrence Reid, maltman in Perth, 14 Feb. 1776.(CS16.1.168)

CRAMOND, JOHN.   John Cramond in Glasgow then in Norfolk,
     Virginia, V. Thomas Morgan, brewer in Dundee,
     5 Feb. 1777.   (CS16.1.170)

CRAWFORD, DAVID.   David Crawford in St Eustatia V. creditors
     of David Crawford of Crawfordtown, 5 Mar. 1779.
                                              (CS16.1.175)

CRAWFORD, GEORGE.   George Crawford, merchant in Virginia, &
     William Veitch, merchant in Dunfermline, V. Janet
     Veitch, only child of Alexander Veitch, merchant in
     Dunfermline, 9 Mar. 1769.   (CS16.1.134)

CRAWFORD, GEORGE.   George Crawford, merchant in Glasgow
     then in Jamaica, V. Andrew Crawford in Fearlinebank,
     7 Aug. 1777.   (CS16.1.171)

CRAWFORD, JANET.   Janet Crawford, widow of James Simpson,
     merchant in Glasgow then in Grenada, V. the Burgh of
     Ayr, 30 Nov. 1779.   (CS16.1.177)

CROCKATT, JAMES.   James and John Crockatt, George Seaman,
     merchants in Charleston, South Carolina, & Charles
     Crockatt, merchant in Edinburgh, V. Grizell Ross, wife
     of John Ross of Blackhill, & Christian Ross, wife of
     Charles Hay of Hopes, 2 Nov. 1739.   (CS16.1.69)

CROCKATT, JAMES.   James and John Crockatt, George Seaman,
     merchants in Charleston, South Carolina, & Charles
     Crockatt, merchant in Edinburgh, V. Andrew Ross,
     clothier in Musselburgh, 17 Jan. 1739.   (CS16.1.69)

CROCKATT, JAMES.   James Crockatt in Charleston, South
     Carolina, V. Rev. Mathew Reid in Prestonkirk,
     11 July 1741.   (CS16.1.70)

CROCKATT, JOHN.   John Crockatt, merchant in Charleston,
   South Carolina, V. Anna Jaffrey at Northwaterbridge,
   Pert, 18 Dec. 1754.   (CS16.1.95)

CROSS, DAVID.   David Cross of Glenduffhill, merchant in
   Glasgow then in Jamaica, V. William Gardner, shop-
   keeper in Glasgow, 3 Aug. 1779.   (CS16.1.177)

CUMMING, ROBERT.   Robert Cumming, merchant in Virginia, &
   William Cumming, skinner in Kilmarnock, V. John Glen,
   merchant in Glasgow, 5 Aug. 1763.   (CS16.1.115)

CUNNINGHAM, DANIEL.   Daniel Cunningham in St Kitts, son of
   Robert Cunningham of Cayonne, St Kitts, V. Thomas
   Forbes of Waterton, 29 Jan. 1745.   (CS16.1.75)

CUNNINGHAM, GEORGE.   George Cunningham, son of Henry
   Cunningham, surgeon in Edinburgh then in St Augustine,
   East Florida, V. John Cunningham of Balbougie,
   3 Mar. 1772.   (CS16.1.148)

CUNNINGHAM, HENRY.   Dr Henry Cunningham,physician in
   Edinburgh then in East Florida, & Moses Buchanan of
   Glens, V. Esther Cunningham, daughter of George
   Cunningham, surgeon in Edinburgh, 9 Feb. 1769.
                                              (CS16.1.134)

CUNNINGHAM, HENRY.   Henry Cunningham, surgeon in Edinburgh
   then in Florida, V. Stewart Stephen & Scott, merchants
   in Leith, & Walter Hogg, clerk to the British Linen
   Company, 3 Mar. 1770.   (CS16.1.141)

CUNNINGHAM, WILLIAM.   William Cunningham, merchant in
   Falmouth, Virginia, then in Glasgow, V. George Kerr,
   merchant in Williamsburg, Virginia, & Hugh Kerr,
   sheriff substitute of Renfrew, 7 July 1768. (CS16.1.133)

CURRIE, DAVID.   David Currie in New York, George McCree in
   New York, etc. V. John Tait, 16 Dec. 1781. (CS16.1.181)

CURRIE, ROBERT.   Robert and Walter Currie in Providence,
   Rhode Island, V. Thomas Leslie, writer in Linlithgow,
   1 July 1738.   (CS16.1.68)

CUTHBERT, JOSEPH. Joseph Cuthbert, son of James Cuthbert,
    physician in Georgia, Lewis and George Cuthbert in
    Jamaica, Roger Cuthbert, son of Lauchlan Cuthbert in
    French Service, James Cuthbert in Georgia - representatives
    of George and Alexander Cuthbert of Castlehill, V.
    Lieutenant Colonel Hugh Grant of Moy, 8 Mar. 1783.
                                                    (CS17.1.2)

DALLAS, WALTER. Walter Dallas, merchant in Baltimore,
    Maryland, V. James Dallas, only child of George Dallas,
    eldest son of James Dallas, eldest son of George Dallas
    of St Martins, 11 Dec. 1754.   (CS16.1.95)

DALLAS, WALTER. Walter Dallas, merchant in Baltimore,
    Maryland, and his children Clere, Ann, Sarah, Elizabeth,
    Nathan and Rachel, & Robert Dallas, surgeon in
    Kingston, Jamaica, V. James Dallas, 29 July 1756.
                                                    (CS16.1.99)

DALLAS, NATHAN. Nathan, Ann, Rachel, and Katherine Reid,
    children of Walter Dallas, merchant in Edinburgh then
    in Baltimore County, Maryland, V. Alexander Dallas, silk
    dyer in Edinburgh, 21 July 1773.   (CS16.1.157)

DALRYMPLE, DAVID. Dr David Dalrymple in St Kitts V. Anne,
    Countess of Balcarres, 22 Dec. 1780.   (CS16.1.181)

DALRYMPLE, DAVID. Dr David Dalrymple in St Kitts, V. the
    Earl of Balcarres, 4 Dec. 1781.   (CS16.1.185)

DALRYMPLE, JANET. Janet Dalrymple, wife of William
    Aitchison in Markinch, sister of David Dalrymple in
    St Kitts, V. Alexander, Earl of Balcarres, 29 July 1772.
                                                    (CS16.1.151)

DANSKINE, JAMES. James Danskine, merchant in Stirling then
    in Florida, V. Alexander Hutton, shoemaker in Stirling,
    4 Aug. 1780.   (CS16.1.181)

DAVIDSON, ALEXANDER. Alexander Davidson, bookseller in
    Edinburgh then in Inverness, V. William Backshelf,
    merchant in London, & Captain Joseph Avery re settlement
    in South Carolina, 9 Mar. 1739.   (AC7.44.287)

DAVIDSON, ANDREW. Andrew Davidson, merchant in Paisley
    then in Virginia, V. James Davidson, merchant in Paisley,
    28 Nov. 1764.   (CS16.1.120)

DAVIDSON, GEORGE.   George Davidson, surgeon in Tobago, &
    James Davidson, merchant in Paisley, V. James
    Davidson, writer in Paisley, 4 Dec. 1776.   (CS16.1.170)

DAVIDSON, GEORGE.   George Davidson of Lowisdale, surgeon in
    the West Indies, V. Thomas Story, merchant in London,
    13 July 1779.   (CS16.1.175)

DEANS, JEAN.   Jean Deans, servant in Barbados, V. William
    Ovens, servant to John Hood in Trows, 21 Nov. 1783.
                                                   (CS17.1.2)

DEAS, DAVID.   David and John Deas, & James and William
    Lennox, merchants in Charleston, South Carolina, V.
    Monro Ross of Pitcalnie, 5 July 1775.   (CS16.1.165)

DENNY, JAMES.   James Denny in America, son of James Denny,
    schoolmaster in Greenock, etc. V. John Murdoch,
    merchant in Glasgow, 9 July 1778.   (CS16.1.173)

DEWAR, MARGARET.   Margaret Dewar, daughter of Robert Dewar,
    merchant in Antigua, V. John Morton, tenant farmer in
    Drumcross, 28 Nov. 1778.   (CS16.1.173)

DICK, JOHN.   John Dick, carpenter in Airth, V. James
    Addison, merchant in Bo'ness, re the voyage of the
    Christian from Airth to Virginia during 1772.   (AC7.55)
                                                     (AC7.55)

DICK, WILLIAM.   William Dick, merchant in Dundee the captain
    of the ... Regiment of Foot in the West Indies, V.
    Charles McGlashan in Fingarth, 28 Feb. 1781.(CS16.1.183)

DICKSON, JOHN.   John Dickson in Salem, Jamaica, V. William
    Dickson, brewer in Lasswade, 24 June 1778. (CS16.1.173)

DICKSON, JOHN.   John Dickson in Hanover, Jamaica, V.
    Archibald and Alexander Brown, farmers in Carrington,
    11 Mar. 1780.   (CS16.1.179)

DICKSON, WILLIAM.   William Dickson of Whitslaid, carpenter in
    Kingston, Jamaica, V. his brother Michael Dickson and his
    sister Janet Dickson, wife of Thomas Ritchie in Whitslaid,
    and their children James and Ann Ritchie, 6 Aug. 1776.
                                                 (CS16.1.170)

DICKSON, WILLIAM.   William Dickson of Whitslaid in Kingston,
    Jamaica, V. Rev. David Dickson and his eldest son William,
    & John Dickson of Kilbucho, 14 Jan. 1777.   (CS16.1.170)

DOIG, ANNE.   Anne Doig, only child of William Doig in
    Antigua, V. Archibald Stevenson, 28 Jan. 1783.(CS17.1.2)

DONALD, ROBERT.   Robert Donald, merchant in Warwick,
    Virginia, V. Anne and Margaret Donald, the younger
    children of James Donald, merchant in Greenock,
    22 July 1778.   (CS16.1.173)

DONALDSON, JAMES.   James Donaldson, son of James
    Donaldson, merchant in Maryland, V. Colin McLauchlan,
    tenant farmer in Bannachrine, 15 July 1748. (CS16.1.80)

DONALDSON, JAMES.   James Donaldson, eldest son of James
    Donaldson, merchant in Annapolis, Maryland, second son
    of James Donaldson of Murroch, and Bridget Donaldson,
    widow of the said James Donaldson merchant, and Henry
    Donaldson, captain of the Lee, third son of said James
    Donaldson of Murroch, V. William Donaldson of Murroch,
    Nov. 1749.   (CS16.1.81)

DONALDSON, ROBERT.   Robert Donaldson, shipmaster in New York
    then in St Andrews, V. Colonel Alexander Monypenny of
    Pitmilly, 4 July 1765.   (CS16.1.122)

DONALDSON, WILLIAM.   William Donaldson, eldest son of James
    Donaldson, merchant in Annapolis, Maryland, second son
    of James Donaldson of Murroch, & Colin McLachlan in
    Bannacbrae, Dunbartonshire, V. William Donaldson of
    Murroch, eldest son of James Donaldson of Murroch,
    26 July 1739.   (CS16.1.69)

DOUGLAS, ALEXANDER.   Alexander Douglas, preacher in
    Carolina, John Stevenson, merchant in Bo'ness, etc. V.
    David Adie, writer in Dunfermline, 3 Jan. 1752.
                                                 (CS16.1.88)

DOUGLAS, ARCHIBALD.   Archibald Douglas, son of James
    Douglas, merchant in Virginia, V. Archibald Douglas of
    Douglas, etc., 13 Dec. 1775.   (CS16.1.165)

DREW, ROBERT.   Robert Drew in Maryland, executor of John
    Drew, merchant in Glasgow, V. Young, Auchincloss & Laing,
    merchants in Glasgow, 2 July 1776.   (CS16.1.168)

DRUMMOND, JOHN.   John Drummond & James McLauchlan in Cecil
    County, Maryland, & James Neilson, merchant in Glasgow,
    V. James Drummond, merchant in Edinburgh, 15 Dec. 1748.
                                                 (CS16.1.80)

                            21

DRUMMOND, JOHN.   John Drummond & James McLauchlan,
    merchants in Cecil County, Maryland, James Neilson,
    merchant in Glasgow, & Hew Milliken, merchant in Port
    Glasgow, V. James Buchanan, merchant in Glasgow,
    7 Feb. 1750.   (CS16.1.84)

DRUMMOND, ROBERT.   Robert Drummond, eldest son of John
    Drummond, excise supervisor in Avoch, Fortrose, then
    in Kingston, Jamaica, V. Thomas Drummond in
    St Ninians, 2 Dec. 1778.   (CS16.1.174)

DUFF, WILLIAM.   William Duff, merchant in the island of
    Rattan, America, V. Alexander Brodie of Brodie,
    26 Nov. 1751.   (CS16.1.85)

DUN, JAMES.   James Dun, merchant in Maryland & Jamaica, V.
    Abigail Dun, daughter of John Dun writer in Edinburgh,
    24 Dec. 1760.   (CS16.1.107)

DUNBAR, GEORGE.   George Dunbar, merchant in Edinburgh then
    in New York, V. William Fettes, merchant in Edinburgh,
    24 Jan. 1783.   (CS17.1.2)

DUNBAR, HELEN.   Helen and Elizabeth Dunbar, sisters of
    John Dunbar, merchant in Sunberry, Georgia, children
    of George Dunbar of Leuchold, V. Edward Tyson, merchant
    in London, 29 Nov. 1769.   (CS16.1.138)

DUNBAR, JOHN.   John Dunbar, physician in Antigua, only
    son of Charles Dunbar in Antigua, & Gratianas Hart,
    only child of John Hart, counsellor-at-law in Antigua,
    and his wife Grace Dunbar, daughter of the said
    Charles Dunbar, V. Charles Warner Dunbar, 21 July 1779.
                                                   (CS16.1.175)

DUNCAN, ALEXANDER.   Alexander Duncan, merchant in
    Wilmington, Carolina, & the other trustees of Michael
    Ancrum, merchant in Edinburgh, V. Henrietta Hay, widow
    of Thomas Murray, shipmaster in Leith, 26 Nov. 1763.
                                                   (CS16.1.117)

DUNCAN, ANDREW.   Andrew Duncan, merchant in Glasgow then in
    New England, John Duncan, brushmaker in Glasgow then in
    Maryland, William Duncan in Glasgow then in Norfolk,
    Virginia, Thomas Duncan, bookseller in North America,
    Robert Duncan, bookseller in Glasgow, V. Isabel Duncan,
    daughter of William Duncan, bookseller in Glasgow,
    30 Nov. 1774.   (CS16.1.161)

DUNCAN, CHARLES. Charles Duncan in New York, David Duncan,
merchant in Dundee, etc, V. Patrick Hill, tenant farmer
in Inchmichael, 5 July 1776.   (CS16.1.168)

DUNCAN, CHARLES. Charles Erskine Duncan, only son of
Charles Duncan in New York, and his tutor David Duncan,
merchant in Dundee, V. Helen Pearson, widow of Captain
Patrick Graeme, son of Ludovick Graeme of Inchbrakie,
6 Mar. 1779.   (CS16.1.175)

DUNCAN, DAVID. David Duncan, gunsmith in Charleston, South
Carolina, & James Cockburn, hair merchant in Edinburgh,
V. Robert Savage, wigmaker & hair merchant in Edinburgh,
7 Aug. 1779.   (CS16.1.177)

DUNCAN, JOHN. John Duncan, merchant in Maryland, Andrew
Duncan, merchant in Worcester, & William Duncan,
printer in Norfolk, Virginia, V. David Dale, merchant
in Glasgow, 1 Mar. 1777.   (CS16.1.170)

DUNCAN, JOHN. John Duncan, merchant in Maryland, & William
Duncan, printer in NOrfolk, Virginia, V. James
Donaldson, merchant in Glasgow, etc, 3 July 1777.
                                          (CS16.1.171)

DUNCAN, MARGARET. Margaret Duncan, wife of George Gordon,
wright in Aberdeen then in Jamaica, & James Gordon,
merchant in Aberdeen then in Jamaica, V. George Moir
of Scotstoun, 20 Nov. 1782.   (CS17.1.1)

DUNCAN, THOMAS. Thomas Duncan, merchant in Philadelphia, &
John Menzies & John Stewart, merchants in London, V.
James Chrisp & Francis Warren, merchants in London,
15 July 1767.   (CS16.1.130)

DUNCAN, THOMAS. Thomas Duncan, merchant in Philadelphia,
John Menzies & John Stewart, merchants in London, V.
Bell & Rannie, merchants in Leith, 10 Dec. 1767.
                                          (CS16.1.130)

DUNCAN, THOMAS. Thomas Duncan, bookseller in Glasgow then
in North America, V. Isabel Duncan, daughter of William
Duncan, bookseller in Glasgow, 7 Aug. 1776. (CS16.1.170)

DUNCAN, THOMAS. Thomas Erskine Duncan, son of Charles
Duncan in New York, V. Ann Duncan, only sister of
Charles Duncan, etc, 18 Feb. 1779.   (CS16.1.175)

23

DUNCAN, WILLIAM.   William Duncan, merchant in Glasgow then
     in New England, Thomas Duncan, bookseller in North
     America, & John Duncan, brush manufacturer in Glasgow
     then in Maryland, V. Isabel Duncan in Glasgow, daughter
     of William Duncan, bookseller in Glasgow, 11 Feb. 1778.
                                                    (CS16.1.173)

DUNCAN, WILLIAM.   William Duncan, bookseller in Glasgow
     then in America, Thomas Duncan, army suttler in New York,
     John Duncan in America, Andrew Duncan, planter in
     Massachusetts, V. Alexander Kincaid, 19 July 1780.
                                                    (CS16.1.179)

DUNLOP, ARCHIBALD.   Archibald Dunlop, merchant in Glasgow
     then in Virginia, V. David and Alexander Campbell,
     merchants in Glasgow, 9 Dec. 1766.   (AC7.51)

DUNLOP, ARCHIBALD.   Archibald Dunlop and .... Ralston,
     merchants in Virginia then in Glasgow, V. David Dalyell
     and George Oswald, merchants in Glasgow, 22 Feb. 1769.
                                                    (CS16.1.134)

DUNLOP, JAMES.   James Dunlop, merchant in Glasgow then in
     North America, V. George Goldie, manager of the British
     Linen Company, 5 July 1769.   (CS16.1.134)

DUNLOP, JAMES.   James Dunlop, merchant in Glasgow then in
     Virginia, V. Glasgow Kingstreet Shoe & Tanning Company,
     1 July 1767.   (CS16.1.130)

DUNLOP, JAMES.   James Dunlop, merchant in Glasgow then in
     America, V. James, Robert, and Isobel Ewing, children
     of James Ewing, mason in Greenock, 8 July 1772.
                                                    (CS16.1.151)

DUNLOP, JAMES.   James Dunlop, merchant in Glasgow then in
     America, V. Coutts Brothers & Company, merchants in
     London, 13 July 1769.   (CS16.1.138)

DUNLOP, JAMES.   James Dunlop, merchant in Glasgow then in
     Virginia, Andrew Donald, merchant in Greenock, etc., V.
     Brown, Yuill & Company, merchants in Glasgow, 31 July
     1772.   (CS16.1.151)

DUNLOP, JAMES.   James Dunlop, merchant in Virginia then in
     Glasgow, V. Thomas Peter & William Bogle, merchants in
     Glasgow, 22 Feb. 1769.   (CS16.1.134)

DUNLOP, JAMES.   James Dunlop, merchant in Glasgow then in
    Virginia, V. Colin and Thomas Dunlop, Alexander Houstoun
    & James Ritchie, merchants in Glasgow, & Colin Rae,
    merchant in Little Govan, 1 Mar. 1769.   (CS16.1.134)

DUNLOP, JAMES.   James Dunlop, merchant in Glasgow then in
    North America, V. Archibald & William Coats, merchants
    in Glasgow, 9 Mar. 1769.   (CS16.1.134)

DUNLOP, JAMES.   James Dunlop, merchant in Glasgow then in
    Virginia, V. George Carmichael & Company, merchants
    in Glasgow, 22 June 1769.   (CS16.1.134)

DUNLOP, JAMES.   James Dunlop, merchant in Glasgow then in
    North America, V. John Browning, tenant farmer in
    Brocklardyke, 9 Mar. 1770.   (CS16.1.141)

DUNLOP, JAMES.   James Dunlop, merchant in Glasgow then in
    North America, V. Patrick Montgomerie, shipmaster in
    Irvine, 9 Mar. 1770.   (CS16.1.141)

DUNLOP, JAMES.   James Dunlop, merchant in Glasgow then in
    America, etc, V. Walter Monteith & Company, merchants
    in Glasgow, 10Mar. 1774.   (CS16.1.157)

DUNLOP, JAMES.   James Dunlop, merchant in Glasgow then in
    Virginia, V. Robert Marshall, merchant in Glasgow,
    27 July 1774.   (CS16.1.161)

DUNLOP, JAMES.   James Dunlop, merchant in Glasgow then in
    Virginia, V. John Carlyle & Company, merchants in
    Glasgow, 9 Feb. 1775.   (CS16.1.161)

DUNLOP, JAMES.   James Dunlop, merchant in Glasgow then in
    America, V. Robert Arthur, merchant in Irvine, 5 July
    1769.   (CS16.1.134)

DUNLOP, JAMES.   James Dunlop of Garnkirk,merchant in
    Glasgow then in Virginia, V. Monteith & Company,
    merchants in Glasgow, 15 June 1776.   (CS16.1.168)

DUNLOP & RALSTON.   Dunlop & Ralston, merchants in Virginia,
    David Conchie, master of the _Betsy of Glasgow_, etc, V.
    Herries, Cochrane and Company, merchants in Glasgow,
    7 Aug. 1767.   (CS16.1.130)

25

DUNMORE, ROBERT. Robert Dunmore and Company, merchants in
Glasgow, V. William Davies Quarrel in Hanover, Jamaica,
21 Nov. 1780 (AC7.57)

EASON, ROBERT. Robert Eason, merchant in Stirling, V.
Robert Kerr, master of the Quebec of Greenock, re a
voyage to Quebec, 13 Dec. 1782. (AC7.58)

EDGAR, JAMES. James Edgar, planter in St Mary's, Jamaica, &
Margaret, widow of Alexander Edgar of Netherhouse, V.
John Mather, merchant in Kingston, Jamaica, then in
Hamilton, 1 Dec. 1779. (CS16.1.177)

EDINBURGH & JAMAICA SHIPPING COMPANY. Edinburgh & Jamaica
Shipping Company V. Robert McClellan, merchant in Leith,
13 Aug. 1754. (AC7.46.130)

EDMONSTONE, WILLIAM. William Edmonstone in Jamaica V. John
Campbell, writer in Stirling, 8 Feb. 1774. (CS16.1.157)

EISTON, JOHN. John Eiston, writer in Edinburgh, V. John
Armstrong, writer in Edinburgh then in Jamaica, 30 June
1778. (AC7.56)

ELLIOT, JOHN. John Elliot in Quebec then in Jamaica,
Thomas Ainslie, merchant in Quebec, & James Potts,
writer in Jedburgh, V. John Strettill, merchant in
London, 10 Feb. 1780. (CS16.1.179)

ELMSLEY, ALEXANDER. Alexander Elmsley in Carolina then in
London V. James Young, son of James Young of Nethersfield,
merchant in North Carolina, & Andrew Millar, merchant
in North Carolina, 23 Feb. 1780. (CS16.1.179)

ERSKINE, JOHN. John Erskine, planter in Jamaica, V. George
Home of Branxton, 1 Feb. 1782. (CS16.1.185)

ERSKINE, JOHN. John Erskine, planter in Jamaica, V. Douglas
Herron and Company, 9 Mar. 1782. (CS17.1.1)

EUSTACE, HANCOCK. Hancock Eustace in Virginia, and his wife
Isobel Blair, sister of John Blair, merchant in Edinburgh,
V. William Hog, merchant in Edinburgh, 8 July 1763.
(CS16.1.115)

EUSTACE, JOHN. John Eustace, physician in New York, V. Anne
Pringle, widow of Colonel John Young, 46th Regiment,
21 Feb. 1767. (CS16.1.126)

26

FAIRHOLM, THOMAS.   Thomas Fairholm, merchant in Edinburgh
    then in Tobago, V. George Fairholm of Greenhill,
    10 Dec. 1776.   (CS16.1.170)

FAIRHOLM, THOMAS.   Thomas Fairholm, merchant in Edinburgh
    then in Tobago, V. Joseph Forrest, writer in Dunbar,
    25 Feb. 1779.   (CS16.1.175)

FAIRLEY, JAMES.   James Fairley, merchant in Virginia then in
    Pensacola, V. William Muir, eldest son of Dr William Muir
    in Kilmarnock then in North America, 24 Jan. 1781.
                                               (CS16.1.181)

FALCONER, WILLIAM.   William Falconer, Governor of York Fort,
    Hudson Bay, V. James, Earl of Fife, 23 Nov. 1776.
                                               (CS16.1.170)

FERGUSON, HUGH.   Hugh Ferguson in North America, David
    Cochrane of the Virginia Coffee House, London, etc, V.
    Douglas Heron and Company, bankers in Ayr, 9 Dec. 1778.
                                               (CS16.1.174)

FERGUSON, ROBERT.   Robert Ferguson, merchant in Virginia
    then in Ayr, V. John CHalmers and Company, merchants
    in Glasgow, 24 June 1772.   (CS16.1.148)

FERGUSON, ROBERT.   Robert Ferguson, storekeeper in Maryland,
    & Murdoch Murchie, innkeeper in Minniaive, V. Andrew
    Ferguson in Minniaive, 19 July 1774.   (CS16.1.161)

FINLAY, THOMAS.   Thomas Finlay in Barbados V. Thomas
    Bethune of Kilconquhar, 22 July 1736.   (CS16.1.66)

FISHER, ADAM.   Adam Fisher, merchant in New York, son of
    James Fisher, merchant in Inveraray, James Fisher,
    merchant in Inveraray, & Angus Fisher, merchant in
    Inveraray then in Pinimore, V. John and Robert Elain,
    merchants in Leeds, 12 June 1755.   (CS16.1.95)

FISHER, ADAM.   Adam Fisher, merchant in New York, V. Neil
    Campbell of Duntroon, & Colin McLaughlan of Craignetance,
    2 July 1766.   (CS16.1.125)

FISHER, ADAM.   Adam Fisher, mariner in New York, & Angus
    Fisher, merchant in Inveraray, sons of Provost James
    Fisher, merchant in Inveraray, V. Captain James Campbell
    in Inveraray, 19 Feb. 1772.   (CS16.1.148)

27

FISHER, JAMES. James Fisher in Jamaica V. Robert Marshall,
    distiller in Grangehall, 1 Feb. 1782. (CS16.1.185)

FLEMING, DAVID. David Fleming, merchant in Edinburgh then
    in South Carolina, Lauchlane McBean, vintner in
    Edinburgh, etc, V. James Edmonstone of Crichtn, 10 Feb.
    1773. (CS16.1.154)

FLEMING, GARDNER. Gardner Fleming, merchant in Suffolk,
    Virginia, V. George Anderson, John Ingram, & John Blair,
    merchants in Glasgow, 12 Dec. 1764. (CS16.1.120)

FLEMING, JOHN. John Fleming, printer in Boston, & Alexander
    Fleming, manufacturer in Newliston, V. John Boyne,
    typefounder in Edinburgh, 3 July 1770. (CS16.1.141)

FORBES, ALEXANDER. Alexander Forbes, merchant in Philadelphia
    Pennsylvania, son of James Forbes in Badyfurrow, V.
    William Murray, merchant in Aberdeen, 16 Feb. 1748.
                                              (CS16.1.80)

FORSYTH, JOHN. John Forsyth, former mate of the John of
    Glasgow then in North America, V. Robert Crawford,
    merchant in Glasgow, 25 June 1783. (CS17.1.2)

FOTHERINGHAM, GEORGE. Dr George Fotheringham, physician in
    Jamaica, Robert Fotheringham of Bandeen, etc, V.
    Archibald Ogilvie of Inchmartine, 14 July 1772.
                                              (CS16.1.151)

FRASER, DONALD. Donald Fraser in Carolina, son of Donald
    Fraser, tacksman of Fishertown of Petty, V. Margaret
    Clerk, wife of David Fraser in Torbreck, 12 June 1767.
                                              (CS16.1.126)

FRASER, JAMES. James Fraser in Jamaica V. Robert Marshall,
    distiller in Grangehall, 1 Feb. 1782. (CS17.1.1)

FRASER, JOHN. John Fraser, shipbuilder in Ayr, John Smith,
    shipmaster in Ayr, & James Montgomery, tacksman, V.
    Robert Ferguson of Castlehill, and David Cochran,
    merchant in Virginia, 1 Aug. 1777. (AC7.56)

FREEBAIRN, DAVID. David Freebairn, merchant in Kingston,
    Jamaica, & William Noble, shipmaster in Port Glasgow,
    V. Thomas Crawford, merchant in London, 3 July 1767.
                                              (AC7.52)

FRIGG, ANDREW. Andrew Frigg, shipmaster in Jamaica, Hugh,
Alexander, David, John, and Katherine, all children of
John Frigg, merchant in Findhorn, V. Thomas Sommers,
vintner in Edinburgh, 22 Feb. 1780. (CS16.1.179)

FRIGG, ROGER. Roger Frigg, eldest son, and Marie Frigg,
only daughter of Andrew Frigg, shipmaster in Jamaica,
V. Thomas Sommers, vintner in Edinburgh, 10 Dec. 1777.
(CS16.1.171)

GALBRAITH, JAMES. James Galbraith, baker in Glasgow then
in Quebec, son of John Galbraith, V. John Galbraith of
Ardfinlay, 29 July 1773. (CS16.1.154)

GALBRAITH, JOHN. John Galbraith of Ardfinlay in North
America V. James McFarlane, schoolmaster in Port of
Menteith, 29 July 1778. (CS16.1.174)

GALBRAITH, PETER. Peter Galbraith, storekeeper in North
Carolina then in Glasgow, V. Charles Reid & Company,
Merchants in Greenock, 6 Mar. 1778. (CS16.1.173)

GALBRAITH, THOMAS. Thomas Galbraith, merchant in New York,
V. Alexander Sangster, linen weaver in London, 26 Feb.
1777. (CS16.1.170)

GALL, ROGER. Roger Gall, merchant at the Bay of Honduras,
V. William Campbell, Principal Clerk of the High Court
of Admiralty, 21 Nov. 1781. (CS16.1.184)

GARDEN, ALEXANDER. Alexander Garden, merchant in Boston, V.
Walter Orroch, merchant in Methil, 5 July 1754.
(AC7.46.101)

GEDDIE, BARBARA. Barbara Geddie, wife of John Imrie, shipbuilder in Carolina, V. John Pitcairn & David Simson,
merchants in Dundee, 8 Mar. 1766. (CS16.1.125)

GERMISTOUN, HARRY. Harry Germistoun in Strichen, Orkney,
then in Virginia, V. William Honeyman of Grahamsay,
7 Nov. 1741. (CS16.1.70)

GIBSON, HELEN. Helen Gibson, wife of Francis Russell,
Surgeon General to the Army in America, V. Walter
Colville, baker in Edinburgh, 5 Aug. 1760. (CS16.1.107)

GILCHRIST, JOHN.   John Gilchrist, carpenter on the
    Benjamin of the Bay of Honduras, V. Roger Gale,
    merchant at the Bay of Honduras, 24 Apr. 1778.   (AC7.56)

GILCHRIST, WILLIAM.   William Gilchrist, merchant in Kilmarnock,
    V. James Dunlop, merchant in Glasgow, re cargo of the
    Agnes from Virginia, 28 June 1765.   (AC7.51)

GILLESPIE, JOHN.   John Gillespie, shipmaster in Boston, V.
    John Hamilton, clerk to the Excise yacht Royal George
    of Leith, 3 Aug. 1774.   (CS16.1.161)

GILMOUR, ROBERT.   Robert Gilmour, merchant in Paisley then
    in Maryland, V. William Jamieson, merchant in Paisley,
    22 July 1772.   (CS16.1.151)

GILMOUR, ROBERT.   Robert Gilmour, merchant in Maryland,
    William Forsyth, merchant in Virginia, Airy & Gilmour,
    merchants in Maryland, Robert Blair, merchant in Boston,
    & Turnbull & Shaw, merchants in Virginia, V. John
    Telfer, merchants in Glasgow, 6 Mar. 1778.   (CS16.1.173)

GLEN, JAMES.   James Glen of Longcroft, Advocate General of
    Carolina, & Captain Walter Hamilton of Westport, V.
    Jean Broun, Lady Colstoun, 27 June 1746.   (CS16.1.78)

GLEN, JAMES.   James Glen of Longcroft, former Governor of
    South Carolina, etc, V. John, Elizabeth, and Graham
    Forbes, children of Hugh Forbes, Clerk of Session,
    10 Feb. 1773.   (CS16.1.154)

GLEN, WALTER.   Walter Glen, weaver in Paisley then in Boston,
    John Baird, mariner on the Peggy of Glasgow, George
    Ramsay in North Carolina, & Robert Wilson in Philadelphi,
    V. the trustees of Robert Crawford, merchant in Glasgow,
    19 June 1771.   (CS16.1.146)

GLENNIE, JAMES.   James Glennie in Jamaica, son of Thomas
    Glennie, merchant in Aberdeen, V. William Nicol,
    advocate in Aberdeen, 11 Dec. 1776.   (CS16.1.170)

GOLDIE, GEORGE.   George Goldie, manager of the British Linen
    Company, V. the executors of Dr William Horseburgh in
    New Providence, 6 Dec. 1763.   (AC7.50)

GOLDPAP, JAMES.   James Goldpap in New York then in London,
    V. Hugh McLean, paymaster of Major Allan McLean's
    battalion of foot, 30 June 1772.   (CS16.1.151)

GORDON, ALEXANDER.   Alexander Gordon, merchant in Boston,
    V. Alexander McConnochie, 21 Jan. 1761.   (CS16.1.107)

GORDON, ALEXANDER.   Rev. Alexander Gordon in Glasserton then
    in Maryland, V. James Stewart, 5 Dec. 1770. (CS16.1.143)

GORDON, ALEXANDER.   Alexander Gordon in Tobago, representative
    of his brother Charles Gordon, writer in Edinburgh then
    in Tobago, V. James Saunders, 6 Aug. 1778.   (CS16.1.174)

GORDON, ALEXANDER.   Alexander Gordon of Kingsgrange,
    customs collector in Montserrat, V. Elizabeth,
    McLellan, widow of Charles Hunter in Grenada,
    21 June 1781.   (CS16.1.183)

GORDON, ALEXANDER.   Alexander Gordon of Kingsgrange,
    customs collector in Montserrat, & Anthony Gordon,
    planter in Dominica, V. William Campbell, 16 July 1783.
                                                    (CS17.1.2)

GORDON, ALEXANDER.   Alexander Gordon, customs collector in
    Montserrat, brother of Colonel Patrick Gordon of
    Kingsgrange, V. Thomas Durie, merchant in the Isle of
    Man, 2 July 1783.   (CS17.1.2)

GORDON, CHARLES.   Charles Gordon, writer in Edinburgh then
    in Grenada, V. Charles Butter, 10 Mar. 1780.(CS16.1.179)

GORDON, FRANCIS.   Francis Gordon, merchant in Yecomico,
    Virginia, son of Sir Robert Gordon of Earlston, V.
    William Donald, merchant in Ayr, 14 Feb. 1759.(CS16.1.103)

GORDON, JAMES.   James Gordon, merchant in Newfoundland then
    in Aberdeen, V. William Morison, merchant in Greenock,
    1 Dec. 1779.   (CS16.1.177)

GORDON, JAMES.   James Gordon of Corestoun, merchant in
    Stromness then in Georgia, V. John Baikie, excise
    collector in Kirkwall, 30 Dec. 1777.   (CS16.1.171)

GORDON, JAMES.   James Gordon, merchant in Stromness then in
    Georgia, V. James Riddoch, customs collector in Kirkwall,
    18 Feb. 1778.   (CS16.1.173)

GORDON, JAMES.   James Gordon jr, merchant in Stromness
    then in Savannah, Georgia, V. Peter Loutit, merchant
    in Stromness, 1 July 1778.   (CS16.1.173)

GORDON, JAMES.   James Gordon jr, merchant in Stromness
    then in Savanna, Georgia, V. Edward Irving of Quoylie,
    merchant in Stromness, 1 July 1778.   (CS16.1.173)

GORDON, JOHN.   John Gordon, Captain of an Independent
    Company in New York, V. Alexander Gordon of Cairnfield,
    eldest son of John Gordon, 23 June 1763.   (CS16.1.115)

GORDON, JOHN.   John Gordon, merchant in Virginia, son of
    George Gordon, merchant in Aberdeen, V. George
    Middleton of Seton, 5 Feb. 1766.   (CS16.1.125)

GORDON, ROBERT.   Robert Gordon, planter in St Vincent, V.
    Alexander Gordon of Kingsgrange, 9 July 1783. (CS17.1.2)

GOURLAY, JOHN.   John Gourlay, merchant in Dundee then in
    Carolina, V. Rev. John Williamson in Dundee, 22 Jan.
    1740.   (CS16.1.69)

GOURLAY, WILLIAM.   William Gourlay, merchant in Boston, etc,
    V. Moses Alexander, merchant in London, 10 Feb. 1769.
                                                 (CS16.1.134)

GRAEME, ANNE.   Anne Graeme, widow of David Graeme, in
    Charleston, South Carolina, V. David Graeme, advocate,
    30 June 1780.   (CS16.1.179)

GRAHAM, JOHN.   John Graham of Dougldston in Grenada V.
    Alexander Houston & Company, merchants in Glasgow,
    30 Dec. 1777.   (CS16.1.171)

GRAHAM, PATRICK.   Patrick Graham of Redford in Georgia V.
    David Graham of Whitehill, 16 July 1755.   (CS16.1.95)

GRAHAM, RICHARD.   Richard Graham, merchant in New York, John
    Thomson, merchant in New York, Thomas Aitchison,
    merchant in Virginia, Thomas Farquhar, merchant in
    Edinburgh then in Virginia, Alexander Home in St Kitts,
    James Baird, merchant in Virginia, James Riddell,
    merchant in Guadaloupe, John Park, merchant in Virginia,
    James Turner, merchant in Virginia, & Joseph Corbet,
    merchant in Virginia, V. James Dunlop of Garnkirk,
    merchant in Glasgow, 23 Feb. 1782.   (CS17.1.1)

GRAINGER, HELEN.   Helen Grainger, daughter of James
    Grainger, physician in St Kitts, V. Dr James Hay,
    30 Nov. 1782.   (CS17.1.1)

GRAINGER, LOUISA. Louisa, Agnes, and Ellen Grainger,
    children of Dr James Grainger in St Kitts, V. John
    Williamson of Clerkington, 17 Dec. 1772. (CS16.1.151)

GRANT, ANDREW. Andrew Grant in Grenada V. John Veitch,
    marble cutter in Edinburgh, 30 June 1779. (CS16.1.175)

GRANT, CHARLES. Charles Grant, son of William Grant of
    Glenbeg, merchant planter in Grenada, John Grant,
    writer in Edinburgh then in Jamaica, etc, V. Colquhoun
    Grant, 11 Aug. 1778.   (CS16.1.174)

GRANT, JOHN. John, Allan, Robert, Charles, Margaret,
    Katherine, Ann, and Isabella Grant, children of Andrew
    Grant, merchant in Edinburgh then in Grenada, V.
    Alexander Grant, writer in Edinburgh, 23 Feb. 1781.
                                                  (CS16.1.183)

GRANT, WILLIAM. William Grant, Regimental Quartermaster in
    America, son of Ludovick Grant of Lelloch, & Peter
    Campbell in America, son of Alexander Campbell in
    Ettrish, V. Patrick Anderson in Bellyheglish, 24 Feb.
    1779.   (CS16.1.175)

GRAY, ALEXANDER. Alexander Gray, drover in Sutherland
    then in Carolina, & Lieutenant John Gray V. Douglas
    Gilchrist, factor to the Earl of Sutherland,
    21 Jan. 1761.   (CS16.1.107)

GRAY, ANDREW. Andrew Gray in America, brother of John Gray,
    portioner of Wester Gartshore, V. William Gray, portioner
    of Wester Gartshore, 19 Feb. 1745.   (CS16.1.78)

GRAY, ARCHIBALD. Archibald Gray & John King, merchants in
    Glasgow, V. John Buchanan, merchant in Glasgow, re a
    voyage to Virginia, 16 Apr. 1734.   (AC7.40.137)

GRAY, GEORGE. George Gray, eldest son of Alexander Gray,
    surgeon with the British Legion in America, V. Robert
    Whitehead, wright in the Canongate, 6 Feb. 1783.
                                                   (CS17.1.2)

GRAY, JOHN. John Gray, merchant in Quebec, V. George,
    John, Alexander, and Margaret Gray, children of
    Alexander Gray, 7 Mar. 1781.   (CS16.1.183)

GRAY, ROBERT.   Robert Gray in Jamaica V. John Sutherland
   of Pitgruidie & William Sutherland, writer in
   Edinburgh, 10 Mar. 1773.   (CS16.1.154)

GRAY, WILLIAM.   William Gray of Herboreal, late Provost Marshal
   of Jamaica, V. Janet Sutherland, widow of George Sinclair
   of Brabster, 29 Nov. 1776.   (CS16.1.170)

GRAY, WILLIAM.   William Gray, late Provost Marshal of
   Jamaica now of Skelbo, etc, V. John Carter, late
   Governor of Bengal, 29 July 1780.   (CS16.1.181)

GRAY, WILLIAM.   William Gray of Herboreal, late Provost
   Marshal of Jamaica then in Skelbo, Sutherland, V.
   Hugh Inglis, late in Calcutta, 15 Jan. 1782. (CS17.1.1)

GREENLEES, JAMES.   James, Mary, and Grizel Greenlees,
   children of John Greenlees, merchant in Virginia, and
   his wife Mary Beveridge, & John Monro, merchant in
   Edinburgh, husband of the said Mary Greenlees, V. the
   Royal Bank of Scotland, 26 Feb. 1782.   (CS17.1.1)

GREENLEES, JOHN.   John Greenlees & Thomas Hardy, merchants
   in Norfolk, Virginia, V. Thomas Dunmore & Company,
   merchants in Glasgow, 3 June 1766.   (AC7.51)

GUTHRIE, MOLLY.   Molly Guthrie in Kingston, Jamaica, V.
   John and Hugh Parker, merchants in Kilmarnock,
   24 July 1779.   (CS16.1.175)

HAMILTON, ALEXANDER.   Alexander Hamilton in Maryland and
   North Carolina V. Frances, Gavin, William, Elizabeth,
   Jacobina, and Grizel Hamilton, children of John
   Hamilton of Kype, writer in Mauchline, 10 Mar. 1780.
                                                (CS16.1.179)

HAMILTON, ALEXANDER.   Alexander Hamilton in Maryland,
   eldest son of John Hamilton of Kype, V. William,
   Charlotte, and Grizel Hamilton, children of John
   Hamilton of Kype, 5 July 1782.   (CS17.1.1)

HAMILTON, ARCHIBALD.   Archibald Hamilton, merchant in
   Glasgow then in America, & John Hamilton, merchant in
   Virginia, V. Agnes Peadie, daughter of James Peadie of
   Reichill & James Coulter, merchants in Glasgow,
   10 Aug. 1776.   (CS16.1.170)

HAMILTON, ARCHIBALD.   Archibald Hamilton of Overton, merchant
   in Virginia, & John Hamilton, merchant in Virginia, V.
   Ursula Hamilton, widow of John Smith, surgeon in
   Greenock, 27 Feb. 1778.   (CS16.1.173)

HAMILTON, ARCHIBALD.   Archibald Hamilton, merchant in
   Virginia, V. John Hunter in America, 14 July 1779.
                                                    (CS16.1.175)

HAMILTON, GAVIN.   Gavin Hamilton, merchant in Norfolk,
   Virginia, V. William Hamilton, merchant in London, &
   John Gray, 18 Dec. 1776.   (CS16.1.170)

HAMILTON, GAVIN.   Gavin Hamilton, merchant in Virginia, V.
   William Colquhoun of Kenmore, 4 Dec. 1777. (CS16.1.171)

HAMILTON, JAMES.   James Hamilton, merchant in Boston, New
   England, V. Alexander McKenzie, merchant in Barbados,
   & Sir Hew Dalrymple in North Berwick, 13 June 1753.
                                                     (CS16.1.89)

HAMILTON, JAMES.   James Hamilton, ,etc, V. Morrison, Taylor
   & Company, merchants in Greenock, re the voyage of the
   Rae Galley to the Isle of Lewis, Philadelphia, the
   West Indies, and back to Greenock, 16 Apr. 1776.(AC7.55)

HAMILTON, JAMES.   James Hamilton, factor to Campbell of
   Shawfield, in Islay then in America, V. Douglas Heron
   & Company, bankers in Ayr, 20 Jan. 1779.   (CS16.1.174)

HAMILTON, PRIMROSE.   Primrose Hamilton, daughter of John
   Hamilton in Jamaica, V. the appointed factors &
   tutors, 8 Feb. 1780.   (CS16.1.179)

HAMILTON, STEWART.   Stewart Hamilton in Chiltern Castle,
   Kent, then in North America, James Reid in Edinburgh
   then in North America, etc, V. Alexander Kincaid, His
   Majesty's Printer, 5 Aug. 1778.   (CS16.1.174)

HAMILTON, GOODISONS & COMPANY.   Hamilton, Goodisons and
   Company, merchants in Glasgow & Virginia, V. their
   creditors, 27 Nov. 1778.   (CS16.1.174)

HARRIS, ROBERT.   Robert Harris in Philadelphia, brother of
   William Harris, merchant in Ayr, V. Margaret Halliday,
   milliner in Kirkcudbright, 10 July 1771.   (CS16.1.146)

HARTLEY, RICHARD.   Richard Hartley, master of the
    St George of Montrose, V. Thomas Douglas, merchant
    in Montrose, re a voyage to Africa and Antigua,
    25 June 1754.   (AC7.46.51)

HASTIE, JOHN.   John Hastie, shipmaster of the Hawk of
    Greenock, V. Samuel Lord, mate of the Jolly Tar of
    Piscataqua, New Hampshire, 15 Sep. 1780.   (AC7.57)

HASTIE, JOHN.   John Hastie, shipmaster of the Hawk of
    Greenock, V. Abraham Newell, mate of the Lively of
    Massachusetts, 11 Aug. 1780.   (AC7.57)

HASTIE, ROBERT.   Robert Hastie, merchant in Glasgow then in
    New York, & Henry Lochhead, merchant in Glasgow then in
    the West Indies, etc, V. James Marshall, 4 July 1781.
                                                    (CS16.1.183)

HENDERSON, JOHN.   John Henderson in Jamaica V. William
    Wood of Gallowhill, 15 Nov. 1780.   (CS16.1.181)

HENDERSON, RICHARD.   Richard Henderson in Virginia, Duncan
    Thomson, merchant in Virginia, William Cochran, merchant
    in Glasgow then in Jamaica, James Lyle in Virginia, etc,
    V. Alexander Ross, 12 July 1780.   (CS16.1.179)

HENDRIE, ARCHIBALD.   Archibald Hendrie, merchant in Jamaica,
    & David Hendrie, merchant in St Martins, West Indies,
    sons of James Hendrie, merchant in St Kitts, V.
    Jonathan Anderson, merchant in Glasgow, 4 Dec. 1782.
                                                    (CS17.1.1)

HENDRY, JEAN.   Jean Hendry, widow of Alexander McKay,
    planter in North Carolina, & Neil McGeachy, late in
    Wilmington, North America, V. Flora Hendry, widow of
    Donald McAlister in Arran, 11 July 1783.   (CS17.1.2)

HENDSHAW, JOHN.   John Hendshaw, merchant in Glasgow then in
    New York, V. William Brown jr, merchant in Glasgow,
    9 July 1755.   (CS16.1.95)

HENRY, JAMES.   James Henry, merchant in Havanna, V.
    William Little, writer in Edinburgh, 15 Jan. 1774.
                                                    (CS16.1.155)

HEPBURN, JAMES. James Hepburn and Joseph Montford,
    merchants at Cape Fear and Halifax, North Carolina,
    Thomas Braidwood, book-keeping teacher in Edinburgh,
    etc, V. John Alston, merchant in Glasgow, 9 Dec. 1774.
                                            (CS16.1.161)

HERIOT,GEORGE.   George Heriot, planter in South Carolina,
    V. John Heriot, Sheriff Clerk of Haddington, 31 July
    1771.   (CS16.1.146)

HEUGH, ANDREW.   Andrew Heugh, merchant in Virginia, V.
    Alexander Girdwood, merchant in Glasgow, 21 Feb. 1771.
                                            (CS16.1.143)

HOAKEFLY, ROBERT.   Robert Hoakefly, merchant in New York,
    V. John Blackwood, Lieutenant in 21st Regiment of Foot,
    27 Nov. 1782.   (CS17.1.1)

HODGZART, WILLIAM.   William Hodgzart, merchant in New York,
    John Alison, merchant in St Kitts, V. Alston, Cormalt
    & Company, merchants in Greenock, 8 Feb. 1783.(CS17.1.2)

HOGG, JAMES.   James Hogg, blacksmith in Glasgow then in
    Carolina, etc, V. John Hogg, weaver in Glasgow,
    20 Jan. 1768.   (CS16.1.133)

HOGG, JAMES.   James Hogg, smith in America, son of James
    Hogg, blacksmith in Provan Mill, and his wife Elizabeth
    Stark, V. his brother William Hogg, wright, 19 Dec. 1770.
                                            (CS16.1.143)

HOOD, JOHN.   John Hood, merchant in Virginia, V. Marion and
    Ann Speirs, daughters of John Speirs, merchant in
    Greenock, Jan. 1752.   (CS16.1.88)

HOOD, JOHN.   John Hood, merchant in Virginia then in
    Greenock, V. Andrew Crawford, mariner, 21 Feb. 1764.
                                            (CS16.1.117)

HOOK, JOHN.   John Hook, merchant in Virginia, V. James
    Gemmill, merchant in Greenock, 29 June 1774.(CS16.1.161)

HOWES, ... Howes in Carolina, son of Jacob Howes and
    ..... Goodlate, daughter of James Goodlate of Abbots-
    haugh, V. James Goodlate of Abbotshaugh, 24 June 1740.
                                            (CS16.1.69)

HUNTER, DAVID   David Hunter, merchant in Ayr then in
Virginia, V. Alexander Kennedy, merchant in Ayr,
29 Dec. 1769.   (AC7.53)

HUNTER, JOHN.   John Hunter in America V. Archibald Hamilton,
merchant in Virginia, 14 July 1779.   (CS16.1.179)

HUTCHISON, DANIEL.   Daniel Hutchison, shipmaster in New
York, great grandson of Robert Tennant, shoemaker at the
Water of Leith, V. Alexander Young, brewer in Potterrow,
18 July 1752.   (CS16.1.88)

HUTTON, CHARLES.   Charles Hutton, merchant in Glasgow then
in Maryland, Alexander Thain, merchant in Leith, etc, V.
John and William Graham, wine-coopers in Leith, 18 Dec.
1767.   (CS16.1.130)

HUTTON, JAMES.   James Hutton, tobacconist, William Blyth,
tailor, & Robert Bryson, shipmaster, all in Leith, V.
Gustavus Sinclair, Samuel Welsh, & Archibald Balfour,
merchants in Edinburgh, re the voyage of the Ann of
Edinburgh to Boston, 31 Jan. 1738.   (AC7.43.493)

HYSLOP, WILLIAM.   William Hyslop in Brooklyn, Suffolk
County, Massachusetts, & William Stirling, merchant in
Glasgow, V. John Simson, New London, Connecticut, the
Naval Officer in St Vincent, on behalf of his brothers
Mathew Simson and Joseph Chew in New London, Connecticut,
9 July 1772.   (CS16.1.151)

IMBRIE, JAMES.   James Imbrie, merchant in Falkland then in
New York, V. James Fisken, merchant in Perth, 29 July
1778.   (CS16.1.174)

INNES, FRANCES.   Frances Innes, widow of Alexander Innes,
surgeon in St Kitts, Henry Crook Innes, mariner in the
East Indies, George Innes, surgeon of the 83rd Regiment,
sons of the said Alexander Innes, V. Thomas Kirkpatrick,
merchant in Alexandria, Virginia, brother of William
Kirkpatrick of Raeberry, Kirkcudbrightshire, 7 July 1779.
                                                (CS16.1.175)

INNES, FRANCES.   Frances Innes, widow of Alexander Innes,
surgeon in St Kitts, & Thomas Kirkpatrick, merchant in
Virginia, V. Alexander Maxwell, surgeon in London,
8 Aug. 1782.   (CS17.1.1)

INNES, JOHN.   John Innes of Leuchars, Captain in the Royal
American Regiment, V. Elizabeth Gordon, 8 Dec. 1756.
                                                (CS16.1.99)

IRVINE, CHARLES.   Charles Irvine in Tobago V. David
    Wardrope, surgeon in Edinburgh, 4 July 1783.   (CS17.1.2)

IRVING, THOMAS.   Thomas Irving, Receiver General of South
    Carolina, husband of Marion Corbet, and Robert, Edward,
    and Marion Corbet, children of James Corbet, merchant
    & late Provost of Dumfries, V. George Paton, innkeeper
    in Crawfordjohn, 6 Aug. 1774.   (CS16.1.161)

JAMIESON, JAMES.   James Jamieson, surgeon in Tobago, V.
    Herdman, Buchanan & Company, merchants in Greenock,
    23 July 1783.   (CS17.1.2)

JAMIESON, NEIL.   Neil Jamieson, merchant in Norfolk,
    Virginia, V. Charles Addison & Son, merchant in Bo'ness,
    2 Feb. 1776.   (CS16.1.168)

JAMIESON, NEIL.   Neil Jamieson, merchant in Virginia, James
    Glassford, merchant in Virginia, William Robertson,
    merchant in Antigua, John Glassford, merchant in
    Glasgow, etc, V. William McDowal of Castle Semple,
    20 Dec. 1776.   (CS16.1.168)

JAMIESON, WILLIAM.   William Jamieson, merchant in Virginia,
    Neil Buchanan, merchant in Virginia, John Fisher,
    merchant in Virginia, etc, V. Andrew Houston of
    Calderhill, 30 June 1780.   (CS16.1.178)

JOHNSTON, ANDREW.   Andrew Johnston, merchant in Virginia
    then in Greenock, V. Robert Barclay, writer in Glasgow,
    28 July 1750.   (CS16.1.84)

JOHNSTON, EDWARD.   Edward Johnston in Virginia V. Neil
    Buchanan of Auchintoshan, & John Buchanan, merchant in
    Glasgow, 20 Jan. 1774.   (CS16.1.157)

JOHNSTON, JOHN.   John Johnston, merchant in Norfolk,
    Virginia, son of John Johnston, merchant in Glasgow, &
    John Spreull of Milton, & John Morrison, schoolmaster
    in Old Kirkpatrick, V. Jean Wilson, widow of Aula
    McAula, maltman in Dunbarton, 3 Nov. 1748.   (CS16.1.80)

JOHNSTON, JOHN.   John Johnston in America, & John Melville,
    merchant in Dunbar, V. Gilbert Richardson, innkeeper
    in Langholm, 2 Mar. 1773.   (CS16.1.154)

JOHNSTON, JOHN.   John Johnston in America, David Edgar in
    Reddings, & Andrew Johnston at Burn, V. George Blair of
    Beltonmount, 9 Aug. 1774.   (CS16.1.161)

JONES, WILLIAM. William, Hugh, Marion, Jean, and Susannah
     Jones, children of Dr Hugh Jones, physician in Jamaica,
     & Janet Mein, V. Lieutenant Robert Mein, 1st Regiment
     of Foot, 12 Feb. 1783.   (CS17.1.2)

KEIR, PATRICK. Rev. Patrick Keir on St James Island, South
     Carolina, V. Andrew Bennet of Balgonar & Robert
     Hamilton, merchant in Edinburgh, 16 Jan. 1761.
                                                  (CS16.1.107)

KEMP, JOHN. John Kemp, merchant in Antigua, V. Peter
     Dobson, merchant in Glasgow, 7 Aug. 1782.   (CS17.1.1)

KENNAN, ROBERT. Robert Kennan, merchant in Virginia,
     William Carruthers, merchant in Dumfries, etc, V.
     Jean Kennan, wife of John Wallace, merchant in Dumfries,
     25 Feb. 1769.   (CS16.1.134)

KENNEDY, JOHN. John Kennedy, shipmaster, & William McCree,
     merchant in Glasgow, V. James Tulloch McFie, etc, re the
     voyage of the Carolina to Guinea & Maryland, 16 Jan. 1770.
                                                    (AC7.53)

KENNEDY, JOHN. John Kennedy, clergyman in Ruthven of
     Badenoch, chaplain to the 71st Regiment in America, V.
     Angus McPherson, son of John McPherson of Inverhall,
     16 June 1780.   (CS16.1.179)

KENNEDY, WALTER. Walter Kennedy in British Service in
     America, eldest son of William Kennedy in Leffanhill,
     V. Mrs Margaret Laurie, 11 July 1759.   (CS16.1.105)

KER, EDWARD. Edward Ker, son of George Ker, merchant in
     Virginia, grandson of Edward Ker, merchant in Irvine, V.
     Thomas Boyd of Pitcon, 6 Dec. 1769.   (CS16.1.138)

KER, GEORGE. George Ker & Company, merchants in Virginia,
     V. John Shortridge, merchant in Glasgow, 5 July 1764.
                                                  (CS16.1.117)

KER, GEORGE. George Ker, merchant in Virginia, Edward Ker,
     merchant in Virginia, Hugh Ker and Isabel Ker, children
     of Edward Ker, merchant in Irvine, and Jean Monro, V.
     Ebenezer Hare, merchant in Bristol, 6 Jan. 1759.
                                                  (CS16.1.103)

KERR, JAMES. James Kerr, merchant in Antigua then in East
     Grange, representative of Kerr & Burles, merchants in
     Antigua, V. William Jackson, writer in Edinburgh,
     9 Dec. 1772.   (CS16.1.151)

KING, JOHN.   John King, merchant in Kingston, Jamaica,
    eldest son of George King, merchant in Paisley, V.
    Robert Paterson, writer in Paisley, 7 July 1779.
                                                    (CS16.1.175)

KINNINGBURGH, JOHN.   John Kinningburgh, wright in Virginia
    then in Kirkintilloch, brother of Robert Kinningburgh,
    merchant in Glasgow, & James Kinningburgh, merchant in
    Glasgow, V. Gavin Black, merchant in Glasgow, 25 July
    1753.   (CS16.1.89)

KIRKPATRICK, THOMAS.   Thomas Kirkpatrick, merchant in
    Alexandria, Virginia, V. Miss Henrietta Kirkpatrick,
    5 Aug. 1779.   (CS16.1.177)

KIRKPATRICK, JAMES.   James Kirkpatrick, merchant in
    Alexandria, Virginia, V. Parker, Hunter & Smith,
    merchants in Kilmarnock, 8 Dec. 1779.   (CS16.1.177)

KIRKPATRICK, THOMAS.   Thomas Kirkpatrick, merchant in
    Alexandria, Virginia, V. Hugh Lawson, merchant in
    Dumfries, 24 Feb. 1779.   (CS16.1.175)

KIRKPATRICK, THOMAS.   Thomas Kirkpatrick in Newton of
    Alexandria, Virginia, V. Robert Hunter, 28 July 1779.
                                                    (CS16.1.177)

KIRKPATRICK, THOMAS.   Thomas Kirkpatrick, merchant in
    Alexandria, Virginia, V. John Gordon, 4 July 1781.
                                                    (CS16.1.183)

KIRKPATRICK, THOMAS.   Thomas Kirkpatrick, merchant in
    Alexandria, Virginia, brother of William Kirkpatrick of
    Raeberryden, V. Hugh and William Lawson, merchants in
    Dumfries, 23 Jan. 1782.   (CS17.1.1)

KIRKPATRICK, THOMAS.   Thomas Kirkpatrick, merchant in
    Alexandria, Virginia, V. Elizabeth Robertson, widow of
    Mungo Buchan, architect, 11 Dec. 1782.   (CS17.1.1)

KIRKPATRICK, THOMAS.   Thomas Kirkpatrick, merchant in
    Virginia, & William Ramsay V. John and Hugh Parker,
    merchants in Kilmarnock, 18 Dec. 1782.   (CS17.1.1)

KIRKPATRICK, WILLIAM.   William Kirkpatrick of Raeberry in
    St Kitts V. Campbell, McNeill & Campbell, merchants
    in Campbelltown, 6 Dec. 1775.   (CS16.1.165)

KNOX, JANET.   Janet and Marion Knox, aunts of James Knox
in Virginia, V. George Crawford, merchant in Glasgow,
5 Dec. 1775.   (CS16.1.165)

KNOX, ROBERT.   Robert, William, and Alexander Knox, merchants
in Virginia, V. William Dunlop, shipmaster in Port
Glasgow, 4 July 1781.   (CS16.1.183)

KNOX, ROBERT.   Robert Knox, merchant in Virginia, heir of
John Knox, carpenter in Port Glasgow, V. William
Dunlop, shipmaster in Port Glasgow, 23 Jan. 1782.
                                                (CS17.1.1)

LAING, JOHN.   John Laing, merchant in Cromarty then in
Maryland, & Archibald Hamilton, merchant in Edinburgh,
V. Matthew Robertson, shipmaster in Bo'ness, 25 July
1740.   (AC7.45.666)

LANG, GEORGE.   George Lang, barber in Glasgow then in
Virginia, V. James Lang, coppersmith in Glasgow,
7 Dec. 1763.   (CS16.1.117)

LAUCHLAND, JEAN.   Jean Lauchland, daughter of Thomas
Laughland, merchant in Boston, New England, V. Janet
Lauchland, wife of George Little in Coltness,
26 Nov. 1751.   (CS16.1.85)

LAURIE, PETER.   Peter Laurie, merchant in Guadaloupe then
in Swinslee, V. David Laurie in Swinslee & John Laurie,
writer in Edinburgh, 2 Mar. 1782.   (CS17.1.1)

LEALL, JOHN.   John Leall in Dinwiddie County, Virginia, &
Kenneth Leall, messenger in Elgin, V. Janet Gordon,
wife of Alexander Duff, in Fochabers, 2 Mar. 1773.
                                                (CS16.1.154)

LEARMONTH, JOHN.   John Learmonth, son of Alexander Learmonth
in Lewiston, Pennsylvania, and nephew of Christian
Learmonth, milliner in Edinburgh, V. Lady Charlotte
Gordon, daughter of Alexander, Duke of Gordon,
26 Feb. 1766.   (CS16.1.125)

LEIGH, AMELIA.   Amelia Leigh, daughter of Austin Leigh,
minister in Dominica, V. James Ramsay, dyer in Pencaitland,
10 Feb. 1780.   (CS16.1.179)

LEITH, JOHN.   John Leith in Tobago V. John Grant of
Rothmaise, 25 June 1782.   (CS17.1.1)

LEITH, ROBERT.   Robert Leith, former baillie of Pittenweem,
     Margaret Leith, widow of John Buchanan of Galstone,
     Samuel Hazard, George Stafford & Alexander Forbes, all
     in Philadelphia, Pennsylvania, V. Archibald and John
     Coats, merchants in Glasgow, 4 July 1751.   (CS16.1.85)

LESLIE, ANDREW.   Captain Andrew Leslie, mariner in London
     then in Antigua, V. Patrick Chrigan, merchant in Newton
     Stewart, & James Gordon of Grange, 3 Jan. 1739.
                                            (CS16.1.68)

LESLY ALEXANDER.   Major General Alexander Lesly, on His
     Majesty's Service in America, V. Sir Robert Laurie of
     Maxwellton, 7 July 1781.   (CS16.1.183)

LEWIS, WILLIAM.   William and Matthew Lewis, planters in
     Jamaica, V. Somerville, Gordon & Company, merchants in
     Glasgow, 26 June 1778.   (AC7.56)

LITHGOW, THOMAS.   Thomas Lithgow, planter in Grenada, Helen
     Lithgow, widow of William Braidwood, candlemaker in
     Edinburgh, & Margaret Lithgow, wife of Ebenezer Gardner,
     linen manufacturer in Edinburgh, V. John Robertson,
     jeweller in Edinburgh, 24 Feb. 1779.   (CS16.1.175)

LIVINGSTONE, MUSCOE.   Captain Muscoe Livingstone in Virginia,
     John Day in London, & Robert Ferguson of Castlehill, V.
     Ronald McDonald, merchant in London, 28 July 1772.
                                            (CS16.1.151)

LOCHHEAD, HENRY.   Henry Lochhead, merchant in Virginia, Joan
     Semple, wife of John Jamieson, merchant in Glasgow, etc,
     V. John Nasmyth, maltman baillie of Hamilton, 12 July
     1764.   (CS16.1.117)

LOCHHEAD, HENRY.   Henry Lochhead, merchant in Virginia, V.
     John Wilson, eldest son of William Wilson of Unthank,
     10 Aug. 1765.   (CS16.1.125)

LOCHHEAD, HENRY.   Henry Lochhead, merchant in Virginia, V.
     James Syme, baker in Hamilton, 29 Jan. 1766.(CS16.1.125)

LOCHHEAD, HENRY.   Henry Lochhead, merchant in Virginia,
     eldest son of Henry Lochhead, merchant in Glasgow, and
     Elizabeth Semple, V. Marion Brown, widow of John Miller
     of Waterhaugh, etc, 31 Jan. 1766.   (CS16.1.125)

LOCHHEAD, HENRY.   Henry Lochhead, merchant in Alexandria
     then on the James River, Virginia, V. John and James
     Wilson, merchants in Kilmarnock, 9 Aug. 1776.(CS16.1.170)

LOCK, GEORGE.   George Lock in Charleston then in Glasgow
     V. Gavin Lawson, mason in Glasgow, 28 Feb. 1751.
                                             (CS16.1.85)

LOCKARD, HENRY.   Henry Lockard, merchant in Alexandria,
     America, then in Glasgow, V. James Wilson & Son,
     merchant in Kilmarnock, 12 July 1777.   (CS16.1.171)

LOGAN, GEORGE.   George Logan, shipmaster in Philadelphia,
     V. David Muir, maltster in Kilwinning, 18 Nov. 1753.
                                             (CS16.1.103)

LOGAN, GEORGE.   George Logan, sailor in New England,
     nephew of David Logan, writer in Kilwinning, V. Robert
     Dick, Professor of Philosophy in Glasgow, 18 Jan. 1758.
                                             (CS16.1.100)

LOGAN, THOMAS.   Thomas Logan, merchant in Westmoreland
     County, Virginia, V. James Clark, merchant in Kilmarnock,
     15 July 1767.   (CS16.1.130)

LOTHIAN, STEWART.   Mrs Stewart Lothian (sic), wife of
     Andrew Lothian in Edinburgh then in Jamaica, V. Margaret
     Hamilton, wife of James Hamilton of Bangour, 17 Feb.
     1778.   (CS16.1.173)

LOVE, WILLIAM.   William Love, merchant in Virginia, James
     Pettigrew, merchant in Virginia, Alexander Shaw,
     merchant in Virginia, & James Blane, merchant in
     Grenada, V. Patrick Telfer, merchant in Glasgow,
     5 Mar. 1778.   (CS16.1.173)

LOVEL, JOHN.   John Lovel, son of Thomas Lovel, merchant
     in Boston, New England, & William McCunn, shipmaster
     in Greenock, V. John McCulloch, merchant in
     Kirkcudbright then in Liverpool, 23 July 1755.(CS16.1.95)

LUNDIE, ARCHIBALD.   Archibald Lundie, merchant in Savanna,
     Georgia, V. John Buchanan, merchant in Greenock,
     27 Nov. 1781.   (CS16.1.185)

LYLE, JAMES.   James Lyle in Virginia, & John Barbour,
     merchant in Kilbarchan, V. Ludovick Lyle, merchant
     tailor in Port Glasgow, 9 Mar. 1758.   (CS16.1.100)

MALCOLM, DUGALD.   Dugald Malcolm at Pit River, Jamaica, V.
    Duncan Ochiltree of Linsaig, 3 Feb. 1778.   (CS16.1.173)

MANSFIELD, JAMES.   James Mansfield, merchant in Edinburgh,
    V. John Elphinston, merchant in Aberdeen, re the voyage
    to Antigua & Jamaica, 13 Feb. 1756.   (AC7.48.970)

MARGETSON, JAMES.   James Margetson, merchant in London, V.
    Thomas Skinner, mate of the Gustavus of Philadelphia,
    21 Sep. 1781.   (AC7.58)

MARGETSON, JAMES.   James Margetson, merchant in London, V.
    William Gibbons, shipmaster, & Thomas Cleghorn, mate
    of the Four Friends of Boston, 5 Oct. 1781.   (AC7.58)

MARGETSON, JAMES.   James Margetson, merchant in London, V.
    Moses Grinnell, shipmaster of the Beckey and Harriet of
    Boston, 19 Oct. 1781.   (AC7.58)

MARSHALL, JOHN.   John Marshall, merchant in Virginia, etc,
    V. Sir Michael Stewart of Blackhall, 11 July 1772.
                                            (CS16.1.151)

MARSHALL, JOHN.   John Marshall, merchant in Louisa County,
    Virginia, etc, V. David Crawford of Crawfordtoun,
    10 Feb. 1779.   (CS16.1.175)

MARSHALL, WILLIAM.   William Marshall, merchant in Glasgow
    then in the West Indies, V. James Fleming, merchant in
    Glasgow, 19 May 1782.   (CS17.1.1)

MARSHALL, WILLIAM.   William Marshall, merchant in Tobago,
    and his son John Marshall V. John Hart, merchant in
    London, 17 July 1783.   (CS17.1.2)

MATHER, JOHN.   John Mather, merchant in Kingston, Jamaica,
    then in Hamilton, V. James Edgar, planter in St Mary's,
    Jamaica, 3 Feb. 1779.   (CS16.1.174)

MAXWELL, MATTHEW.   Matthew Maxwell, merchant in Virginia &
    Maryland, son of Rev. James Maxwell in Pollockshiells,
    V. Robert Maxwell of Shott, 17 Jan. 1759.   (CS16.1.103)

MEIKLE, JOHN.   John Meikle, surgeon in Jamaica, and Mary
    Meikle in Paisley, children of John Meikle and ....
    Forsyth, Tobias Burke, blockmaker in Greenock then in
    America, V. John Smith, shipmaster in Ayr, James
    Montgomery, tacksman of Newton Coalwork, 17 June 1780.
                                            (CS16.1.179)

MEIKLE, JOHN.   John Meikle, surgeon in Jamaica, V. William
   Fullerton of Rosemount, 14 Nov. 1781.   (CS16.1.184)

MEIKLE, JOHN.   John Meikle, surgeon in Jamaica, V. George
   Gardner of Ladykirk, 22 Jan. 1783.   (CS17.1.2)

MEIKLE, JOHN.   John Meikle, surgeon in Jamaica, V. John
   Smith, baillie of Ayr, 30 July 1783.   (CS17.1.2)

MEIN, JANET.   Janet Mein, daughter of William Mein, and
   wife of Dr Hugh Jones, physician in Edinburgh then in
   Jamaica, V. Marion Mackie, widow of William Mein sr,
   merchant in Edinburgh, 10 July 1782.   (CS17.1.1)

MENZIES, JOHN.   John Menzies, bookseller in Port Glasgow
   then in New York, etc, V. Alexander Kincaid, His
   Majesty's Printer, 7 Aug. 1778.   (CS16.1.174)

MIDDLETON, PETER.   Dr Peter Middleton, physician in New
   York, V. James Turnbull of Corrie, 2 Aug. 1770.
                                               (CS16.1.141)

MIDDLETON, PETER.   Dr Peter Middleton, physician in New
   York, V. James Brown, son of ... Brown, surgeon in
   Dalkeith, and ... Turnbull, 18 Nov. 1772.   (CS16.1.151)

MIDDLETON, PETER.   Dr Peter Middleton, physician in New
   York, deceased, per his executors Andrew Elliot &
   Robert Auchmuty, and Francis Strachan, V. John Scott,
   son of James Scott, druggist in Edinburgh, 1 Feb. 1782.
                                               (CS17.1.1)

MIDDLETON, PETER.   Dr Peter Middleton, physician in New
   York, V. Francis Strachan, 25 Jan. 1783.   (CS17.1.2)

MILLER, DAVID.   David Miller, surgeon in Westmoreland, Jamaica,
   V. William Miller, merchant in Dundee, 8 Mar. 1766.
                                               (CS16.1.125)

MILLAR, GEORGE.   George Millar, leather merchant in
   Edinburgh then in South Carolina, Mrs Telfor in
   Edinburgh, etc, V. John Tawse,writer in Edinburgh,
   17 Jan. 1776.   (SC16.1.168)

MILLER, HUGH. Hugh Miller in Mecklenburg, Virginia, V.
James Johnston in London & Richard Oswald of
Auchencruive, 2 Mar. 1779.   (CS16.1.175)

MILLER, JAMES. James Miller, merchant in Virginia, V.
William Allan, carpenter on the Beverley of Glasgow,
3 June 1774.   (AC7.55)

MILLER, JOHN. John Miller in St John's Island, North
America, now in LOndon, V. William Kirkpatrick, merchant
in Dumfries, 11 Aug. 1780.   (CS16.1.181)

MILLER, ROBERT. Robert Miller, planter in Portland,
Jamaica, then in Tobago, V. James Dalgleish, merchant
in Bo'ness, 15 July 1778.   (CS16.1.173)

MILLER, THOMAS. Thomas Miller in Lord Cathcart's Regiment
in America V. Andrew Story of West Brace, 2 July 1779.
                                          (CS16.1.175)

MILLER, WILLIAM. William Miller, merchant in Virginia then
in Glasgow, V. John Wilson, merchant in Glasgow, 28 July
1749.   (CS16.1.81)

MILLIGAN, DAVID. David Milligan, merchant in New York, V.
Alexander Spiers, merchant in Glasgow, 4 July 1781.
                                          (CS16.1.183)

MIRRYLEES, ALEXANDER. Alexander Mirrylees, brewer in Leith
then in South Carolina, son of John Mirrylees, V.
William Moffat, writer in Edinburgh, 30 June 1779.
                                          (CS16.1.175)

MITCHELL, GEORGE. George Mitchell in Kilmarnock then in
Winchester, Virginia, V. Thomas Johnston, merchant in
Glasgow, 13 July 1768.   (CS16.1.133)

MITCHELL, JOHN. John Mitchell, merchant in Virginia, Hugh
Tran, merchant in St Kitts, V.Rev. Patrick Maxwell in
New Monklands, 31 July 1782.   (CS17.1.1)

MITCHELL, JOHN. John Mitchell, chapman in Penninghame then
in America, V. John Douglas in Brigtoun, 29 Jan. 1783.
                                            (CS17.1.2)

MITCHELL, THOMAS. Thomas Mitchell in Irvine then in New
England, & John Mitchell, sailor in Irvine then in
New England, V. James Wilson, merchant in Kilmarnock,
25 June 1755.   (CS16.1.95)

MOIR, ANN. Ann Moir, sister of Rev. James Moir in
Edgecombe County, North Carolina, wife of Archibald
Murdoch, merchant in Doune, V. Rev. Henry Moir in
Auchtertool, 19 Nov. 1768.   (CS16.1.134)

MOIR, JEAN. Jean Moir, daughter of Henry Moir, merchant in
Doune, sister of Rev. James Moir in Edgecombe County,
North Carolina, wife of James Murdoch, merchant in
Leith, V. Rev. Henry Moir in Auchtertool, 19 Nov. 1768.
                                                   (CS16.1.134)

MONRO, DUNCAN. Duncan Monro, merchant in America, brother
of George Monro of Culcairn, V. John Hodgson in London,
5 July 1782.   (CS17.1.1)

MONTFORD, JOSEPH. Joseph Montford, merchant in North
Carolina, V. John Alston, merchant in Glasgow, 20 Dec.
1775.   (CS16.1.168)

MONTGOMERY, JOHN. John Montgomery, merchant on the James
River, Virginia, & Joseph Glen, shoemaker in Glasgow
then in Nova Scotia, V. William Glen, merchant in
Glasgow, 4 Dec. 1776.   (CS16.1.170)

MOODIE, ROBERT. Robert, John, Helen, Ann, and Rachel Moodie,
children of Thomas Moodie, merchant in Carolina, etc, V.
Robert Hog, merchant in North Berwick, 12 Feb. 1772.
                                                   (CS16.1.148)

MOOR, BENJAMIN. Benjamin Moor, eldest son of William Moor,
joiner in Piscataqua, Ranton River, Middlesex County,
New Jersey, V. Thomas Trotter, brewer in Edinburgh,
16 Dec. 1762.   (CS16.1.114)

MORRIS, STAATS. Staats Lang Morris in New York, and his
wife Katherine, Duchess of Gordon, V. John Gordon,
tenant of the Mill of Boaterie, 8 Mar. 1758.(CS16.1.100)

MOUBRAY, THOMAS. Thomas Moubray, eldest son of Arthur
Moubray, surgeon in South Carolina, V. James Bull of
Cronaster in Shetland, 19 Nov. 1751.   (CS16.1.85)

48

MUIR, ADAM. Adam Muir, merchant in Virginia, V. Thomas
    Muir, vintner in Edinburgh, 24 Nov. 1756. (CS16.1.99)

MUIR, ADAM. Adam Muir, merchant in Virginia, V. Robert
    Wilson, brewer in Newbattle, 16 Feb. 1757. (CS16.1.99)

MUNRO, JOHN. John Munro, advocate procurator fiscal, V.
    William Sextroh, shipmaster of the Minerva of Charleston,
    South Carolina, 19 June 1778.   (AC7.56)

MURE, MARGARET. Margaret Mure, wife of Dr William Bowie,
    physician in Antigua, Helen Mure, wife of ... Hunter,
    merchant in Antigua, etc. V. John Gloag & Company,
    merchants in Edinburgh, 1 July 1779.   (CS16.1.175)

MURRAY, ADAM. Dr Adam Murray, physician in Maryland, V.
    James Summers, writer in Edinburgh, 24 Feb. 1769.
                                               (CS16.1.134)

MURRAY, GEORGE. George Murray in Kingston then in Savanna-
    la-Mar, Jamaica, V. John, Lord Oliphant, in Clarendon
    parish, Jamaica, and Dr David Oliphant, physician &
    planter in Carolina, 27 Feb. 1773.   (CS16.1.154)

MURRAY, JAMES. James Murray, merchant in Leith then in
    Virginia, V. James Murray, merchant in Fraserburgh,
    28 Feb. 1744.   (CS16.1.73)

MURRAY, JAMES. James Murray, writer in Edinburgh then in
    Jamaica, & .... Coomans in Rotterdam V. James Ross,
    writer in Edinburgh, 22 Feb. 1764.   (CS16.1.117)

MURRAY, JOHN. John Murray of Murraywhat, Secretary to the
    Province of Carolina, V. Sir John Douglas, etc,
    20 July 1764.   (CS16.1.117)

MURRAY, THOMAS. Thomas Murray, shipmaster of the Wilmington
    of Cape Fear & Michael Ancrum, merchant in Edinburgh, V.
    William Wemyss, writer in Edinburgh, 15 Nov. 1757.
                                               (CS16.1.100)

MURRAY, WILLIAM. William Murray, shipmaster & merchant in
    New York, V. William Lang, merchant in Glasgow,
    10 Mar. 1764.   (CS16.1.117)

MUSCHET, ROBERT. Robert Muschet in St Elizabeth's, Jamaica,
    & James Colquhoun, merchant in Dunbarton, V. Dunbarton
    Town Council, 15 Dec. 1773.   (CS16.1.154)

MUSCHET, ROBERT.   Robert Muschet, merchant in Jamaica, V.
Alexander Robertson in Jamaica then in Strathardle,
Kirkmichael parish, 7 Dec. 1776.   (CS16.1.170)

MUSCHET, ROBERT.   Robert Muschet of Green, merchant in
Jamaica, V. William King, merchant in Port Glasgow,
29 Jan. 1778.   (CS16.1.173)

MUSCHET, ROBERT.   Robert Muschet, merchant in Jamaica, V.
Henry Campbell in Kilchornan, Islay, 20 Jan. 1779.
                                            (CS16.1.174)

MUTTER, ... Mutter in North America V. Janet Wardrope,
wife of John Muir of Greenhall, 19 Dec. 1782. (CS17.1.1)

McADAM, JOHN.   John Loudoun McAdam, merchant in New York, V.
Gilbert McAdam of Meikland, 23 Nov. 1781.   (CS16.1.184)

McADAM, JOHN.   John Loudoun McAdam, merchant in New York,
Jacobina, Grizel, Elizabeth, Katherine, Wilhelmina,
and Hanna McAdam, children of James McAdam of Waterhead,
& Adam Stewart, merchant in Glasgow, husband of the said
Grizel, V. Gilbert McAdam of Meikland, 1 Aug. 1782.
                                            (CS17.1.1)

McADAM, JOHN.   John Loudoun McAdam, merchant in New York,
eldest son of James McAdam of Waterhead, V. Douglas,
Heron & Company, bankers in Ayr, 6 Feb. 1782.(CS17.1.1)

McALISTER, HECTOR.   Hector McAlister & Robert Donald,
merchants in Norfolk, Virginia, V. Joseph Berwick in
Worcester, 1 July 1778.   (CS16.1.173)

McALISTER, HECTOR.   Hector McAlister & Robert Donald,
merchants in Norfolk, Virginia, Robert Alexander &
Thomas Donald, merchants in Greenock, & James and Robert
Donald, merchants in Glasgow, V. Joseph Berwick in
Worcester, 9 Dec. 1778.   (CS16.1.174)

McALISTER, WILLIAM.   William McAlister, merchant in Virginia,
V. John McKechnie, merchant in Glasgow, 3 Dec. 1769.
                                            (SC16.1.107)

McAUSLAN, ROBERT.   Robert McAuslan, merchant in Glasgow and
Newfoundland, V. Thomas Tait, merchant in Glasgow,
1 July 1783.   (CS17.1.2)

McBEAN, ANGUS.   Angus McBean, merchant in Kingston, Jamaica,
    Ann McBean, wife of Alexander Mann, merchant in Invernes,
    & Katherine McBean, wife of George Shivaz, merchant in
    Inverness, V. Robert Shivaz, shoemaker in Inverness,
    29 Jan. 1778.   (CS16.1.173)

McCALL, JOHN.   John McCall in America, son of Thomas McCall,
    merchant in Glasgow, V. Gershan & Hyam Isaac, merchant
    in London, 6 Aug. 1783.   (CS17.1.2)

McCALL, SAMUEL.   Samuel McCall, clerk to Samuel McCall &
    Company, merchants in Glasgow then schoolmaster and
    planter in Virginia, V. James Wilson, merchant in
    Greenock, 6 Feb. 1765.   (CS16.1.120)

McCANDLISH, WILLIAM.   William McCandlish, miller in Mill of
    Alries then in Janefield, America, V. Patrick McCandlish,
    cartwright in Glasserton, & John McCandlish, carpenter in
    America then in Kerrouchtree, 11 Dec. 1776. (CS16.1.170)

McCAULL, JAMES.   James McCaull, merchant in Glasgow then in
    Virginia, son of Rev. John McCaull in Whithorn, V. John
    McCaull, son of Henry McCaull, merchant in Glasgow,
    2 July 1746.   (CS16.1.78)

McCLURE, GILBERT.   Gilbert McClure & Thomas Cumming,
    merchants in Ayr then in America, V. William Lang,
    merchants in Glasgow, 6 Dec. 1775.   (CS16.1.165)

McCOURTRIE .... McCourtrie in Jamaica V. David Blair,
    customs controller in Dumfries, 29 July 1778.(CS16.1.174)

McCRAE, GEORGE.   George McCrae, merchant in Ayr then in New
    York, V. Jean Hamilton of Bowtreehill, 18 June 1783.
                                                      (CS17.1.2)

McCREE, GEORGE.   George McCree, merchant in Ayr then in
    America, V. John Brown, merchant in Glasgow, 15 Feb. 1780.
                                                     (CS16.1.179)

McCULLOCH, THOMAS.   Thomas McCulloch, merchant in Gosport,
    Norfolk County, Virginia, then in Glasgow, V. Roger
    Stewart, merchant in Portsmouth, Virginia, then in
    Greenock, & Robert Stewart, merchant in Portsmouth,
    Virginia, then captain of the privateer Fincastle,
    6 July 1780.   (CS16.1.179)

McDONALD, ALEXANDER. Alexander McDonald in Tarbet then in
     Virginia, John Ross, merchant in Tain then in
     Philadelphia, Thomas Gally, writer in Edinburgh then in
     Kingston, Jamaica, Margaret Sinclair in Jamaica, daughter
     of Sir James Sinclair of Dunbeath, V. William
     Sutherland, writer in Edinburgh, 7 Aug. 1770.(CS16.1.141)

McDONALD, ARCHIBALD. Archibald McDonald in Inndresh then in
     North America, & Donald McNeil in Gigha then in North
     America V. Dougald McLauchlan, merchant in Fort William,
     5 Feb. 1782.   (CS16.1.185)

McDONALD, JOHN. John McDonald in America, son of James
     McDonald in Riebick, Charles McDonald the younger of
     Kingsburgh, ensign in the Royal Emigrant Regiment in
     America, John Grant jr, writer in Edinburgh then a
     Lieutenant in General Fraser's Regiment, etc, V.
     Duncan McDonald, writer in Edinburgh, 2 Dec. 1778.
                                                     (CS16.1.174)

McDONALD, JOHN. John McDonald, Lieutenant in the 42nd
     Regiment then in the Maryland Loyalists, V. Alexander
     McKay of Moness, 12 Dec. 1781.   (CS16.1.184)

McDOUGALL, ALEXANDER. Alexander McDougall, clerk, V. Robert
     Bailley & John McKenna, merchants in Edinburgh, & Walter
     Scott, shipmaster of the Elizabeth & Peggy of Leith,
     re a voyage to Carolina, 7 Oct. 1757.   (AC7.49.1293)

McDOUGALL, PATRICK. Patrick McDougall in St Kitts then in
     Galleneech, Argyll, V. Malcolm Wright, wireworker in
     Glasgow, 29 June 1780.   (CS16.1.179)

McGHIE, ROBERT. Robert McGhie, eldest son of James McGhie
     in Jamaica, V. Janet Gibson, widow of Captain James Bruce,
     9 Mar. 1774.   (CS16.1.154)

McGILLEVRAY, ALEXANDER. Alexander McGillevray in Charleston,
     South Carolina, then in Petty, Inverness, V. John
     Baillie, 30 June 1738.   (CS16.1.68)

McGILLVRAE, ALEXANDER. Alexander McGillivrae in Carolina
     then in Kelty, Fife, V. Helen and Rebecca Dunbar,
     21 Mar. 1740.   (AC7.45.49)

McGILLIVRAY, ALEXANDER. Alexander McGillivray, merchant in
     Carolina, V. Archibald Dunbar of Newton, 26 July 1743.
                                                      (CS16.1.72)

McGILLIVRAY, ALEXANDER.   Alexander McGillivray, merchant in
    Carolina, V. the heirs of Hugh Fraser of Kinainids,
    9 Feb. 1742.   (CS16.1.70)

McGILLIVRAY, ALEXANDER.   Alexander McGillivray, merchant in
    Carolina, V. Rebecca and Helen Dunbar, daughters of
    Archibald Dunbar of Thunderston, & Archibald Dunbar,
    husband of the said Helen, 15 Jan. 1743.   (CS16.1.72)

McGILLIVRAY, LAUCHLAN.   Lauchlan McGillivray, merchant in
    Charleston, South Carolina, eldest son of William
    McGillivray, brother of Farquhar McGillivray of
    Drumnaglash, V. Farquhar McGillivray of Dalcrombie,
    8 Mar. 1755.   (CS16.1.95)

McGREGOR, ALEXANDER.   Alexander Drummond McGregor in America
    V. John Hall, writer in Edinburgh, 20 July 1780,
                                                  (CS16.1.179)

McGREGOR, ALEXANDER.   Alexander McGregor of Balhalder in
    America V. John Tawse & William McPherson, 13 Feb. 1783.
                                                   (CS17.1.2)

McHARG, JOHN.   John McHarg, son of John McHarg in Glenachie,
    in America V. James McHarg in Fairley, 29 July 1778.
                                                  (CS16.1.174)

McILVAIN, WILLIAM.   William McIlvain, merchant in Philadelphia,
    V. Joseph Gardner, son of William Gardner, writer in Ayr,
    23 Dec. 1767.   (CS16.1.130)

McINTOSH, CHARLES.   Dr Charles McIntosh in Jamaica, George
    Riddoch in London then in Jamaica, & James Huie in Jamaica,
    V. John Gordon, tutor of Elizabeth and Mary Innes,
    daughters of Thomas Innes, 27 Feb. 1782.   (CS17.1.1)

McINTOSH, DANIEL.   Daniel McIntosh, shipmaster in Saltcoats
    then in America, & William Henderson, carter in Orange-
    field, Ediburgh, V. Ann Grant, widow of Robert Reid,
    23 July 1767.   (CS16.1.130)

McINTOSH EDWARD.   Edward McIntosh of Borlum, only son of
    Shaw McIntosh of Borlum, great grandson of William
    McIntosh of Borlum, & the children of ... Ryall, merchant
    in Boston, & the children of ... Palmer, merchant in
    Boston, V. the Duke of Gordon & William Tod, 7 Aug. 1781.
                                                  (CS16.1.184)

McINTOSH, JAMES.   James McIntosh, merchant in Jamaica
then in Farr, Inverness, & John Graham jr, merchant
in Dumfries, V. Arbuthnott & Guthrie, merchants in
Edinburgh, 23 June 1780.   (CS16.1.179)

McIVER, CHARLES.   Charles McIver, bank clerk in Edinburgh
then in Stafford County, Virginia, etc, V. Walter
Ainslie, merchant in Edinburgh, 5 Aug. 1767.(CS16.1.130)

MACKAY, EBENEZER.   Ebenezer Mackay, merchant in Virginia
then in Glasgow, V. James Hunter & Company, merchants
in Ayr, 6 July 1763.   (CS16.1.115)

MACKAY, HUGH.   Colonel Hugh Mackay late in Jamaica V. Ann
Mackay, 30 Nov. 1781.   (CS16.1.184)

MACKAY, HUGH.   Hugh Mackay in Jamaica then in Westfield,
Caithness, V. William Sinclair of Lochend, 5 Aug. 1783.
(CS17.1.2)

MACKAY, PATRICK.   Patrick Mackay in North America V. Major
Alexander Duff, eldest son of John Duff of Cubin,
2 July 1766.   (CS16.1.125)

MACKAY, WILLIAM.   William Mackay & Duff Mackay, merchants in
Inverness, V. Andrew Munroe, merchant in Inverness, &
Daniel Mackay, merchant in London, re a voyage to
Jamaica, 7 June 1734.   (AC7.40.276)

McKEE, ELIZABETH.   Elizabeth McKee, widow of Charles McLeay,
merchant in Newton Stewart then in Jamaica, Judith
McKie, wife of Patrick McHarg, mason in Ferrytown then
in America, etc, V. James Baird, writer in Edinburgh,
4 Feb. 1779.   (CS16.1.174)

McKENZIE, ALEXANDER.   Alexander McKenzie, merchant in
Hampton, Virginia, & James Stewart, writer in Edinburgh,
V. William Napier, shipmaster in Montrose, 16 Feb. 1748.
(CS16.1.80)

McKENZIE, ALEXANDER.   Alexander McKenzie, merchant in Barbados,
James Hamilton, merchant in Boston, New England, heir of
Daniel Hamilton, Chamberlain of Grange, etc, V. .....
Aberdour, 12 Dec. 1753.   (CS16.1.92)

McKENZIE, ALEXANDER.   Alexander McKenzie, merchant in Barbados,
& Sir Hew Dalrymple of North Berwick, V. James Hamilton,
merchant in Boston, New England, 13 June 1753.(CS16.1.89)

McKENZIE, ALEXANDER. Alexander McKenzie & Charles Steuart,
    merchants in Virginia, V. James Fea of Whitehall,
    11 Aug. 1756.   (CS16.1.99)

McKENZIE, ANDREW. Andrew McKenzie, merchant in Boston, V.
    Thomas Hopkirk, merchant in Glasgow, 8 Mar. 1755.
                                                     (CS16.1.95)

MacKENZIE, JAMES. James MacKenzie, former Rector of
    St George, Grenada, V. Hugh McVeagh, son of Hugh McVeagh,
    manufacturer in Huntly, 31 Jan. 1781.   (CS16.1.181)

McKENZIE, JOHN. John McKenzie in Jamaica V. Duncan
    Donaldson of Tulloch, 4 July 1782.   (CS17.1.1)

McKENZIE, MARGARET. Margaret McKenzie, sister of William
    McKenzie, merchant in Glasgow, & Andrew McKenzie in
    the West Indies, nephew of the said William McKenzie,
    V. William Finlayson, writer in Edinburgh, 9 Dec. 1780.
                                                    (CS16.1.181)

McKENZIE, ROBERT. Robert McKenzie in Charleston, South
    Carolina, & James Haig, merchant in Edinburgh, V. John
    Thomson in Jamaica, & Thomas Whitelaw in Jamaica then
    in Glasgow, 8 Mar. 1780.   (CS16.1.179)

McKIE, ISOBELL. Isobell McKie,wife of Captain David
    Johnston of the Marines in Boston, V. William Seaton,
    commander of the **William of Liverpool**, 29 Nov. 1775.
                                                    (CS16.1.165)

MACKIE, THOMAS. Thomas Mackie, saddler in Tanquier County,
    Virginia, V. Thomas Brodie, 4 July 1764.   (CS16.1.117)

MACKIE, THOMAS. Thomas Mackie,saddler in Tanquier County,
    Virginia, V. Robert Donaldson, writer in Edinburgh,
    13 Feb. 1765.   (CS16.1.120)

McKINLAY, PHOEBE. Phoebe McKinlay, sister of Dr Alexander
    McKinlay, in Jamaica then in Leith, V. James Paton,
    wright in Leith, 21 Nov. 1776.   (CS16.1.170)

McKINNON, JOHN. John McKinnon, merchant at the Bay of
    Honduras then in London, V. Roger Gale, merchant at the
    Bay of Honduras, 4 Aug. 1775.   (AC7.55)

McKINNON, JOHN.   John McKinnon, shipmaster in the Jamaica
     trade, V. Roger Gall, merchant at the Bay of Honduras,
     10 Feb. 1778.   (CS16.1.173)

McKINNON, JOHN.   John McKinnon, merchant at the Bay of
     Honduras then in London, V. Roger Gall, merchant in
     Honduras, 2 Aug. 1780.   (CS16.1.181)

McKNIGHT, THOMAS.   Thomas McKnight in Belleville, Curritock
     County, North Carolina, then in Great Britain, V. Hugh
     McMurtrie, shoemaker in Kilmarnock, 31 July 1781.
                                                      (CS16.1.184)

McLACHLAN, JAMES.   James McLachlan & John Drummond,
     merchants in Maryland, V. David Cochran & James
     Buchanan, merchants in Glasgow, 11 Jan. 1749.(CS16.1.80)

McLAREN, JAMES.   James McLaren, watchmaker in Glasgow then
     in Jamaica, & William Gow, watchmaker in Glasgow then
     in St Kitts V. Lewis Allan, writer in Edinburgh,
     14 Feb. 1783.   (CS17.1.2)

McLEAN, DANIEL.   Daniel McLean, merchant in Glasgow then
     in America, V. William Wilson, 13 July 1773.(CS16.1.154)

McLEAN, MURDOCH.   Murdoch McLean, merchant in Edinburgh
     then in America, & Murdoch McLean of Kilmony V. Walter
     McFarlane of Huntsfield, 11 Dec. 1776.   (CS16.1.170)

McLELLAN, ELIZABETH.   Elizabeth McLellan, widow of Charles
     Hunter in Grenada, etc, V. Alexander Gordon of Kings-
     grange, customs collector in Montserrat, 21 June 1781.
                                                      (CS16.1.183)

McLELLAN, JAMES.   James McLellan, surgeon in Balgray House,
     Glasgow, then in Bluefields, St James, Jamaica, William
     McTaggart, surgeon in Gateside of Irongray then in
     Rodapen, Jamaica, V. James Rome in Redkirk, 2 July 1783.
                                                      (CS17.1.2)

McLELLAN, JANET.   Janet McLellan, widow of William Lauder,
     teacher of humanity in Barbados, and daughter of Robert
     McLellan of Summerhall, & her sister Elizabeth McLellan,
     V. Thomas Bryson, brewer in Summerhall, 1 July 1779.
                                                      (CS16.1.175)

McLELLAN, SAMUEL.   Samuel McLellan in Jamaica, son of Robert
    McLellan, merchant in Leith, V. Robert Dryburgh, ship-
    builder in Leith, 9 July 1777.   (CS16.1.171)

McLENNAN, COLIN.   Colin McLennan, printer in Edinburgh then
    in America, etc, V. Alexander Kincaid, 28 July 1779.
                                                  (CS16.1.177)

McLEOD, HUGH.   Hugh McLeod, only son of Robert McLeod, house-
    painter in Maryland, V. Archibald Stewart of Collrain,
    writer in Edinburgh, 8 Dec. 1750.   (CS16.1.84)

McLEOD, HUGH.   Hugh McLeod in Annapolis, Maryland, & George
    Carlyle, merchant in Glasgow, V. Roderick McLeod,
    21 July 1767.   (CS16.1.130)

McLEOD, JOHN.   John McLeod, missionary in Harris then in
    Anson County, North Carolina, John Grant of Pitkerrald,
    Urquhart, now in America, Ninian Menzies, merchant in
    Richmond, Virginia, etc, V. David Ross, accountant in
    Edinburgh, trustee of McPherson & Grant, merchants in
    Edinburgh, 4 Aug. 1775.   (CS16.1.165)

McMATH, JOHN.   John McMath, mariner in New England, V.
    Alexander Cunningham, merchant in Kilmarnock, 1 Feb.
    1741.   (CS16.1.69)

McMICKEN, HUGH.   Hugh McMicken, merchant in Virginia, James
    Hepburn, merchant in Carolina, William McCaa, merchant
    in Virginia, Jefson Welsh & Company, merchants in Cadiz,
    & Patrick Wilson, merchant in Minorca, V. Ebenezer
    McCulloch & Company, merchants in Edinburgh, 13 Feb. 1771.
                                                  (CS16.1.143)

McNAIR, EBENEZER.   Ebenezer McNair, merchant in Glasgow then
    in New York or Long Island, & Alexander Gray, house
    carpenter in Grenada, V. Dunlop & Wilson, merchants in
    Glasgow, 6 Mar. 1781.   (CS16.1.183)

McNEILL, JEAN.   Jean McNeill, wife of .... Rutherford of the
    Loyal Americans, V. Christopher McNeil of Kilchrist,
    21 Feb. 1781.   (CS16.1.183)

McNEIL & CLAXTON.   McNeil & Claxton, merchants in St Kitts,
    Neil McNeil & Company, merchants in Bristol, & John
    Gray, shipmaster in Glasgow, V. John Glassford,
    merchant in Glasgow, 4 Mar. 1756.   (CS16.1.98)

McNEILL, NEILL.   Neill McNeill, merchant in Bristol then in
St Kitts, V. Roger Hamilton McNeill of Taynish, 21 July
1763.   (CS16.1.115)

McNEILL, NEILL.   Neill McNeill, merchant in St Kitts then
in St Croix, V. Devonshire, Rever & Lloyd, merchants in
Bristol, 25 July 1764.   (CS16.1.117)

McNEILL, NEILL.   Neill McNeill, merchant in St Kitts, V.
James Simpson, merchant in Glasgow, 6 Feb. 1765.
                                                        (CS16.1.120)

McNEILL, NEILL.   Neill McNeill, merchant in St Kitts, V.
Colin Campbell of Kilberry, major commandant of the
100th Regiment, 20 Dec. 1764.   (CS16.1.120)

McNISH, JOHN.   John McNish, surgeon in Antigua then in
Glasgow, V. William Bell, shipmaster in Port Glasgow,
2 July 1782.   (CS17.1.1)

McPHERSON, JOHN.   Captain John McPherson of the 17th Regiment
in America, Kenneth McKenzie, soldier in America, Angus
McPherson, soldier in America, Dougald Kennedy, soldier
in General Fraser's Regiment in America, etc., V.
Cuthbert Gordon of Cudbear, manufacturer in Leith,
11 Mar. 1778.   (CS16.1.173)

McPHERSON, JOHN.   John McPherson in Dalwhinnie then in
Jamaica, V. William Shaw, 30 June 1779.   (CS16.1.175)

McQUHAY, ANTHONY.   Anthony McQuhay, merchant in Virginia,
William Alexander, merchant in Antigua, Patrick
Telfer, merchant in Jamaica, James McNeill, merchant in
North Carolina, Andrew Woodrow, merchant in Virginia,
William Gabline, merchant in North Carolina, V. John
Telfer, merchant in Glasgow, 7 Mar. 1778.   (CS16.1.173)

McRAE, WILLIAM.   William and Andrew McRae, merchants in
Virginia, Richard Cogle, merchant in Maryland, James
McMaster, merchant in Boston, Gavin Gilmour & Son,
merchants in Maryland, Walter Robertson, merchant in
Virginia, & Alexander Woddrow, merchant in Virginia, V.
Patrick Telfer, merchant in Glasgow, 3 Mar. 1778.
                                                        (CS16.1.173)

McVICAR, JOHN.   John McVicar in St Thomas-in-the-East,
Jamaica, eldest son of Robert McVicar, excise officer in
Stranraer, and Mary Affleck, only daughter of James
Affleck of Edingham, V. Ebenezer McGeorge of Auchlisk,
2 Feb. 1773.   (CS16.1.154)

McVICAR, JOHN.   John Affleck McVicar in Edingham,
St Thomas-in-the-East, Jamaica, V. John Syme & John
Anderson, 28 Nov. 1782.   (CS17.1.1)

NAPIER, ROBERT.   Robert Napier in Jamaica then in Glasgow
V. William Chisholm in Jamaica then in London,
28 Feb. 1781.   (CS16.1.183)

NASMYTH, JAMES.   Dr James Nasmyth, physician in Jamaica, V.
Robert Nasmyth, eldest son of Robert Nasmyth in
Kirkcudbright, 31 July 1776.   (CS16.1.170)

NASMYTH, JAMES.   Dr James Nasmyth, physician in Jamaica, V.
Robert Nasmyth, eldest son of Robert Nasmyth, eldest son
of James Nasmyth, writer in Edinburgh, 3 Mar. 1778.
                                               (CS16.1.173)

NASMYTH, JAMES.   Dr James Nasmyth, physician in Jamaica, V.
Dunbar, Earl of Selkirk, 16 Feb. 1780.   (CS16.1.179)

NASMYTH, JAMES.   Dr James Nasmyth, physician in Jamaica, V.
Robert Nasmyth, customs collector in Kirkcudbright,
30 June 1781.   (CS16.1.183)

NEILSON, WILLIAM.   William and Hugh Neilson, merchants in
Lewisburg, Virginia, V. John and Hugh Parker, merchants
in Kilmarnock, 6 Dec. 1775.   (CS16.1.165)

NEVAY, JEAN.   Jean Nevay, wife of James Oliphant, goldsmith
in Edinburgh then in America, V. Margaret Nevay in
Edinburgh, 14 July 1780.   (CS16.1.179)

NEWAL, ANDREW.   Andrew Newal, merchant in Westmoreland,
Jamaica, V. Newal & Clark, merchants in Ayr, 10 Mar. 1780.
                                               (CS16.1.179)

NEWMAN, THOMAS.   Thomas Newman, master of the Betsey of
Ipswich, Massachusetts, V. Matthew Squire, captain of
HMS Otter, & James Wardrop, his agent, 1 Nov. 1776.
                                               (AC7.56)

NICOL, JAMES.   James Nicol, merchant in Newport, Rhode
Island, then in Leicester, Worcester County, New
England, V. Isabel Nicol, widow of William Little in
Langholm, 12 Feb. 1766.   (CS16.1.125)

NORRIE, AGNES. Agnes Norrie, wife of William Robertson, surgeon in Jamaica, V. George Norrie, merchant in Dundee, 13 Feb. 1773. (CS16.1.154)

OGILVY, DAVID. Dr David Ogilvy, surgeon in Kingston, Jamaica, then in Aberdeen, V. Colonel Henry Gordon of Knockspeck, 16 Feb. 1782. (CS17.1.1)

OLIPHANT, DAVID. Dr David Oliphant in South Carolina V. John Oliphant, eldest son of John Oliphant of Carpow, 1 Mar. 1775. (CS16.1.165)

OLIPHANT, DAVID. Dr David Oliphant in South Carolina & James Paterson of Carpow V. John Oliphant of Bachilton, LOrd Oliphant, 24 July 1776. (CS16.1.168)

OLIPHANT, DAVID. Dr David Oliphant in Carolina V. David Smyth of Methven, 30 June 1779. (CS16.1.175)

OLIPHANT, JOHN. John Oliphant in Jamaica V. Anne Campbell, widow of Captain John Menzies, 10 Aug. 1773.(CS16.1.154)

OLIPHANT, JOHN. Lord John Oliphant in Jamaica, and his son Captain Henry Oliphant V. Alexander Allan, writer in Edinburgh, 27 Jan. 1773. (CS16.1.154)

OLIPHANT, JOHN. Lord John Oliphant in Jamaica V. Colonel William Mercer of Aldie, 20 Feb. 1782. (CS17.1.1)

ORR, JOHN. John Orr, son of Rev. David Orr in Shotts, storekeeper in Alexandria, Fairfax County, Virginia, V. John Glassford & Archibald Henderson, merchants in Glasgow, 11 July 1770. (CS16.1.141)

OSWALD, RICHARD. Richard Oswald & Alexander Oswald, merchants in Glasgow, V. James Young, master of the Diamond re voyage from the Potomac, 13 July 1739. (AC7.44.488)

OUCHTERLONY, ELIZABETH. Elizabeth Ouchterlony, widow of Patrick Ouchterlony, mariner in Calvert County, Maryland, V. David Mudie, writer in Arbroath, 9 Feb. 1758. (CS16.1.100)

OWENS, THOMAS. Thomas Owens, mariner in Leith then in Jamaica, V. Jean Halliday, wife of George Home, writer in Edinburgh, 26 Feb. 1774. (CS16.1.164)

PAGE, WILLIAM. William Byrd Page, son of William Page
councillor in Virginia, student of physics at the
University of Edinburgh, V. his creditors, 11 July 1778.
(CS16.1.173)

PARK, JOHN. John Park, merchant in Greenock then in
Virginia, V. John Jamieson, merchant in Glasgow,
22 July 1752.   (CS16.1.88)

PARKER, JAMES. James Parker, merchant in Virginia, V.
Janet Thomson, widow of John Lindsay of Balloch,
22 Jan. 1755.   (CS16.1.95)

PARKER, JAMES. James Parker, merchant in Virginia, son of
Patrick Parker, ships carpenter in Port Glasgow, &
William Gordon, merchant in Port Glasgow, V. Margaret
Lindsay, daughter of John Lindsay of Balloch, and her
husband Joseph or Joshua Reid, mariner in Saltcoats,
15 Jan. 1761.   (CS16.1.107)

PARKER, JOHN. John Parker, merchant in Virginia, son of
Patrick Parker, carpenter in Port Glasgow, V. Samuel
Scott, weaver in Greenock, son of John Scott, blacksmith
ther, 9 July 1760.   (CS16.1.107)

PARKER, JOHN. John Parker jr, merchant in Kingston,
Jamaica, etc, V. Parker, Hunter & Smith, merchants in
Kilmarnock, 4 Aug. 1778.   (CS16.1.174)

PATERSON, THOMAS. Thomas Paterson, ropemaker in Leith then
in Maryland, V. Robert Scott, journeyman wright in
Edinburgh, 6 Aug. 1771.   (CS16.1.146)

PATERSON, THOMAS. Thomas Paterson, ropemaker in Leith then
in Virginia, great grandson of Gilbert Story, maltster
in Leith, V. Helen Story, daughter of Gilbert Story,
maltster in Leith, 3 July 1777.   (CS16.1.171)

PATERSON, THOMAS. Thomas Paterson, ropemaker in Leith then
in Baltimore, Maryland, V. Walter McTaggart, ropemaker
in Leith, etc, 16 July 1779.   (CS16.1.175)

PATERSON, THOMAS. Thomas Paterson, ropemaker in Leith then
in Baltimore, Maryland, V. John Scott, exciseman,
25 Feb. 1780.   (CS16.1.179)

PATERSON, WILLIAM. William Paterson in Jamaica, son of
William Paterson in Easter Frew, V. William Galbraith of
Blackhouse, 10 Feb. 1779.   (CS16.1.175)

PEARSON .... Pearson & David Cochrane, merchants in
    Virginia, V. Dunmore, Blackburn & Company, merchants in
    Glasgow, 2 July 1783.   (CS17.1.2)

PEDENE, JAMES.   James Pedene in Virginia, eldest son of
    James Pedene of Mid Auchenlongford, V. Gilbert Innes,
    25 Feb. 1780.   (CS16.1.179)

PENWICK, ... Penwick, widow of Augustus Gwyn, planter
    in St Thomas, Jamaica, Lewis Cuthbert, merchant in
    Kingston, Jamaica, & Thomas Winter, merchant in Spanish
    Town, Jamaica, V. Alexander Houstoun & Company,
    merchants in Glasgow, 3 July 1782.   (CS17.1.1)

PETER, ROBERT.   Robert Peter, merchant in Maryland, V.
    David Peter, shipmaster in Glasgow, 6 Dec. 1775.
                                                   (CS16.1.165)

PETER, WALTER.   Walter Peter & Company, merchants in
    Virginia, V. Josias Corthine, customs collector in Port
    Glasgow, & James Dunlop, merchant in Glasgow, 18 July
    1765.   (CS16.1.122)

PETER, WALTER.   Walter Peter & Company,merchants in Virginia,
    V. Alexander Speirs, Andrew Blackburn, & Andrew Syme,
    merchants in Glasgow, 19 July 1766.   (CS16.1.126)

PETER, WALTER.   Walter Peter, merchant in Virginia, V.
    William Cunningham, merchant in Glasgow, 13 Jan. 1779.
                                                   (CS16.1.174)

PETER, WALTER.   Walter Peter, merchant in Virginia, V.
    Glen & Peter, merchants in Glasgow, 9 Dec. 1778.
                                                   (CS16.1.174)

PETER, WALTER.   Walter Peter, merchant in Virginia, &
    Thomas Dunlop, merchant in Glasgow, V. Dunlop &
    Montgomerie, merchants in Glasgow, 12 Dec. 1781.
                                                   (CS16.1.185)

PETRIE, ALEXANDER.   Alexander Petrie in Antigua, nephew of
    Alexander Petrie, merchant in Elgin, V. Alexander Shaw,
    merchant in Inverness, 30 Dec. 1777.   (CS16.1.171)

PETTIGREW .... Pettigrew in Maryland or Virginia V.
    James Coulter, merchant in Glasgow, 7 July 1779.
                                                   (CS16.1.175)

PETTIGREW, JOHN. James Pettigrew and John Pettigrew in
Virginia, sons of James Pettigrew, merchant in
Virginia, brother of Gavin Pettigrew, wright in
Glasgow, V. John Reid, merchant in Glasgow, 9 Aug. 1780.
(CS16.1.181)

POLSON, HUGH. Hugh Polson in Jamaica, John McKay, planter
in St Thomas-in-the-Vale, Jamaica, V. William McKay in
Bowside, 12 Feb. 1783.   (CS17.1.2)

POTTIE, GEORGE. George Pottie, merchant in Virginia, James
Allan, merchant in Kingston, Jamaica, & John Allan,
merchant in Kingston, Jamaica, V. Mrs Margaret Thomson
in Glasgow, 1 Aug. 1781.   (CS16.1.184)

POTTIE, GEORGE. George Pottie, merchant in Virginia, &
James and John Allan, merchants in Kingston, Jamaica, V.
Mrs Isabel Johnston or Pottie in Kirkcudbright,
23 Nov. 1781.   (CS16.1.184)

POW .... Pow, daughter of Major Theophilius Pow in
Virginia, & Colonel Philip Lightfoot and his son
William Lightfoot in York County, Virginia, V. Andrew
and Archibald Buchanan & Archibald Coats & Company,
merchants in Glasgow, 13 July 1748.   (CS16.1.80)

PRINGLE, ANNE. Anne Pringle, widow of Colonel John Young
of the Royal American Regiment, V. Lord William Napier,
etc, 21 July 1774.   (CS16.1.161)

RAIT, ALEXANDER. Alexander Rait in New England V. John
Shanks, 4 Mar. 1783.   (CS17.1.2)

RAMSAY, GEORGE. George Ramsay in Greenock then in South
Carolina, William Robertson, merchant in Virginia, John
Jamieson, merchant in Charleston, South Carolina, etc, V.
the trustees of Robert Crawford, merchant in Glasgow,
19 June 1771.   (CS16.1.146)

RAMSAY, MARTIN. Martin Ramsay, ensign in the 16th Regiment
in East Florida, V. Katherine Ramsay, wife of William
Davidson, writer in Edinburgh, 28 Jan. 1779.(CS16.1.174)

RAYMER, JAMES. James Raymer, minister in Ponport, South
Carolina, V. James Hunter, James Beveridge, & Edward
Caithness, merchants in Edinburgh, 7 July 1757.
(CS16.1.99)

REID, JAMES.   James Reid, smith in Port Glasgow, V.
     William Miller, shipbuilder in Wilmington, North
     Carolina, 2 Apr. 1776.   (AC7.55)

REID, JOHN.   John Reid, merchant in Carolina, eldest son
     of Captain John Reid, shipmaster in Cromarty, and his
     wife ... Stewart, etc, V. Anne Stewart,wife of Richard
     Newton of Newton, 8 Mar. 1771.   (CS16.1.143)

REID, JOHN.   John Reid, planter in Carriacou, Grenada, V.
     John Rose, tacksman of Horsehill, 8 July 1779.(CS16.1.175)

REID, PATRICK.   Patrick Reid in Waukmill, Tarland, then in
     Antigua, V. James Abercromby of Stank, 8 Aug. 1763.
                                                  (CS17.1.2)

REID, PATRICK.   Patrick Reid in the West Indies then in
     Waukmill, Tarland, V. James Abercromby of Stank,
     23 July 1782.   (CS17.1.1)

REID, THOMAS.   Thomas Reid, merchant in Jamaica, V. John and
     Robert Gordon, writers in Dumfries, 10 Feb. 1779.
                                                 (CS16.1.175)

REID, THOMAS.   Thomas Reid, merchant in Glasgow then in the
     West Indies, V. Coats & Whitelaw, merchants in Glasgow,
     13 June 1783.   (CS17.1.2)

RICHARDSON, DAVID.   David Richardson in Brydekirk then in
     North America, Walter Ball in Stockbriggs then in North
     America, Thomas Henderson, miner in Ecclefechan then in
     North America, & John Crichton in Sanquhar then in North
     America, V. John and Robert Gordon, writers in
     Dumfries, 29 July 1778.   (CS16.1.174)

RIDDELL, GEORGE.   George Riddell, physician in Yorktown,
     Virginia, V. James Riddell in Caister, Norfolk, 7 Dec.
     1763.   (CS16.1.117)

RIDDLE, HENRY.   Henry Riddle in Colchester, Fairfax County,
     Virginia, & John Riddle, merchant in Glasgow, V. Martha
     Dykes, daughter of William Dykes, merchant in Glasgow,
     1 Dec. 1779.   (CS16.1.177)

RIDDOCH, COLIN.   Colin Riddoch, surgeon in Port Royal,
     Virginia, V. Gilbert Laurie, chemist & druggist in
     Edinburgh, 7 July 1756.   (CS16.1.98)

RIDDOCH, COLIN.   Colin Riddoch, physician in Port Royal,
    Carolina County, Virginia, V. The Virginia Company of
    Aberdeen, 13 Jan. 1762.   (CS16.1.114)

RITCHIE, ANDREW.   Andrew Ritchie, merchant in Boston, V.
    Scott & Brown, merchants in Glasgow, 1 Mar. 1769.
                                               (CS16.1.134)

ROBERTSON, ALEXANDER.   Alexander Robertson, James McIver,
    William Malcolm, & Peter Remson, all in New York, &
    Katherine and Ann Ramsay, milliners in Edinburgh, V.
    Alexander Dallas, silk dyer in Edinburgh, 26 July 1769.
                                               (CS16.1.138)

ROBERTSON, ALEXANDER.   Alexander Robertson in Jamaica, his
    wife Margaret Farquharson, only child of James
    Farquharson of Netherelrick, & Robert Muschet, merchant
    in Jamaica, V. James Rattray of Kirkhillocks, 18 Feb.
    1779.   (CS16.1.175)

ROBERTSON, ARCHIBALD.   Archibald Robertson & Patrick
    Robertson, merchants in New London, New England, V.
    George Lind, merchant in Edinburgh, 22 June 1742.
                                               (CS16.1.71)

ROBERTSON, ARCHIBALD.   Archibald Robertson, merchant in New
    London, New England, V. John Snee & Company, merchants
    in London, 15 July 1743.   (CS16.1.72)

ROBERTSON, ARCHIBALD.   Archibald Robertson, merchant in New
    London, New England, the in Appomatix, James River,
    Virginia, V. John Snee & Company, merchants in London,
    5 July 1744.   (CS16.1.75)

ROBERTSON, JAMES.   James Robertson, merchant in America,
    John Robertson, secretary to Admiral Knowles in Russia,
    Jean and Alexander Robertson, children of John Robertson
    of Boghall, V. Andrew Thomson, merchant in Glasgow,
    14 July 1773.   (CS16.1.154)

ROBERTSON, JOHN.   John Robertson, merchant in Glasgow then
    in Virginia, V. Isabel Robertson, daughter of John
    Robertson, writer in Glasgow, 4 Dec. 1754.   (CS16.1.95)

ROBERTSON, JOHN.   John Robertson in Green Island, Jamaica,
    V. Thomas Mitchell in Craig, 2 July 1783.   (CS17.1.2)

ROBERTSON, PATRICK. Patrick Robertson, son of William
    Robertson, merchant in Edinburgh then in New England, V.
    John Barclay, shipmaster & baillie of Dundee, 11 July
    1744.   (CS16.1.75)

ROBERTSON, PATRICK. Patrick Robertson, son of William
    Robertson, baillie of Edinburgh then a merchant in New
    London, New England, V. Arthur Robertson & Archibald
    Hamilton, merchant in Glasgow, 23 Feb. 1742. (CS16.1.70)

ROBERTSON, PETER. Peter Robertson, merchant in Philadelphia,
    V. Andrew Mackie, dyer in Glasgow, 8 Jan. 1740.
                                                    (CS16.1.69)

ROBERTSON, PETER. Peter Robertson, clerk to James Alexander,
    merchant in Edinburgh, then in America, V. James Dewar,
    merchant in Edinburgh, 11 Dec. 1776.   (CS16.1.170)

ROBERTSON, ROBERT. Robert Robertson, merchant in Perth
    then in North America, & ... Van Egmont, merchant in
    Rotterdam, V. Alexander Robertson of Straloch, 1 Aug.
    1776.   (CS16.1.170)

ROBERTSON, ROBERT. Robert Robertson, merchant in Perth
    then in Philadelphia, husband of Mary Stewart, & Mary,
    Charlotte, and Prudence Stewart, children of Robert
    Stewart, deceased, vintner in Perth, V. Duncan
    Donaldson, vintner in Kinross, 10 Mar. 1780.(CS16.1.179)

ROBERTSON, WILLIAM. William Robertson in Crambiny, New Jersey
    V. Jean Kerr, widow of Major Robertson of the Royal
    Dragoons, 12 July 1740.   (CS16.1.69)

ROBISON, WALTER. Walter Robison in Clarendon, Jamaica, V.
    John Oliphant, 2 Mar. 1773.   (CS16.1.154)

ROLLAND, HENRY. Henry Rolland, carpenter in Charleston,
    South Carolina, eldest son of James Rolland, coppersmith
    in Culross, V. William Anderson, carrier & maltman in
    Culross, 9 Mar. 1774.   (CS16.1.137)

ROME, JOHN. John Rome in Jamaica, eldest son of Peter
    Rome in Redkirk, V. George, Marquis of Annandale,
    26 Jan. 1782.   (CS17.1.1)

RONALDSON, ANDREW. Andrew Ronaldson in Wilmington, North
    Carolina, V. John Ronaldson of Blairhall,
    15 Feb. 1783.   (CS17.1.2)

RORISON ROBERT.   Lieutenant Robert Rorison of the 37th
     Regiment of Foot in America V. Scott & Carmichael,
     merchants in Glasgow, 3 Mar. 1778.   (CS16.1.173)

ROSE, ALEXANDER.   Alexander Rose, merchant in Carolina
     then in London, & Hanson, Clark & Company, merchants
     in London, V. Simon Fraser, merchant in London,
     2 July 1767.   (CS16.1.130)

ROSE, CHARLES.   Charles Rose, merchant in Tain then in
     Smithfield, Virginia, & David Ross, town clerk of Tain,
     V. Hugh Ross, silversmith in Tain, 7 June 1776. (AC7.55)

ROSS, ALEXANDER.   Alexander Ross in Mountholly, New Jersey,
     V. Robert Dickson, merchant in Glasgow, 17 Jan. 1770.
                                                  (CS16.1.138)

ROSS, ANDREW.   Andrew Ross V. Charles Crockatt, merchant in
     Edinburgh, James and John Crockatt, James Seaman, & John
     Crockatt jr, merchants in Charleston, South Carolina,
     14 Feb. 1738.   (AC7.43.213)

ROSS, ANDREW.   Captain Andrew Ross of the 31st Regiment of
     Foot in Canada, Isabel Allan, widow of James Ross,
     customs collector in Stranraer. V. Edward Shaw of
     Dunaskine, 18 Aug. 1782.   (CS17.1.1)

ROSS, ANNE.   Anne Ross, wife of Alexander Innes in Aberdeen,
     & Charles Gordon Rose, Elizabeth Hugh Rose, and Anne Rose,
     children of John Rose in Jamaica, V. Charles Gordon of
     Brelach, 15 Jan. 1782.   (CS16.1.185)

ROSS, DANIEL.   Daniel Ross, merchant in Nevis, V. Dr David
     Wardrope of Cults, 2 Dec. 1778.   (CS16.1.174)

ROSS, DAVID.   David Ross, merchant in Baton Rouge, Mississippi,
     and his partners George and Robert Ross V. Veitch &
     Cooper, grocers in LOndon, 11 July 1783.   (CS17.1.2)

ROSS, JOHN.   John Ross, merchant in Tain then in Phila-
     delphia, V. John Duncan, merchant in Dornoch, etc,
     26 Jan. 1764.   (CS16.1.117)

ROSS, JOHN.   John Ross, merchant in Philadelphia V. John
     Sinclair the younger of Fenwick, etc, 16 Feb. 1764.
                                                  (CS16.1.117)

                              67

ROSS, JOHN. John Ross, merchant in London, & James
    McGibbon, brewer in Edinburgh, V. William Dunbar of
    Machriemore in Antigua, 15 Nov. 1765.   (AC7.51)

ROSS, JOHN. Act nominating Isobel Ross, sister of William
    Ross, deceased, in Sleberarass (?), to be curator for
    the children of her brother John Ross, deceased,
    clergyman at Snow Hill, Eastern Shore, Maryland,
    9 Feb. 1780.   (CS16.1.179)

ROSS, JOHN. John Ross, merchant at Loch Broom then in
    Nova Scotia, V. Rev. Joseph Munro in Edertown,
    15 June 1781.   (AC7.58)

ROSS, JOHN. John Ross, merchant at Loch Broom then in
    America, V. Roderick Morrison of Millin, merchant &
    shipmaster in Stornaway, 19 Feb. 1782.   (CS17.1.1)

ROSS, JOHN. John Ross, merchant at Loch Broom then in
    Nova Scotia, V. Alexander Shaw, merchant in Inverness,
    16 Dec. 1783.   (CS17.1.2)

ROSS, PATRICK. Patrick Ross, barber in London then in
    Charleston, South Carolina, V. David Ross in Innerbuist,
    14 July 1779.   (CS16.1.175)

ROSS, WILLIAM. William Ross, merchant at Port Maria Bay,
    St Mary's, Jamaica, V. Stoddart & Fairbairn, wine
    merchants in Edinburgh, 5 July 1780.   (CS16.1.179)

ROSS, WILLIAM. William Ross, merchant in Jamaica, son of
    David Ross in Roslin, V. Walter Ross, 16 July 1783.
                                                   (CS17.1.2)

ROWAND, JOHN. John Rowand, merchant in Glasgow, & Rowand,
    Wills & Rowand, merchants in Charleston, South Carolina,
    V. John Freeman, Thomas Smith & Samuel Smith, merchants
    in Bristol, 23 July 1756.   (CS16.1.98)

ROWAND, WILLS & ROWAND. Rowand, Wills & Rowand, merchants
    in Charleston, South Carolina, V. George Carmichael and
    Company, merchants in Glasgow, 16 Feb. 1757. (CS16.1.99)

ROY, JAMES. James Roy, watchmaker in Falkirk then in
    America, V. Katherine Crawford, widow of James Crawford,
    customs collector in Ayr, 24 June 1779.   (CS16.1.175)

ROYALL, ISAAC.   Isaac Royall, merchant in Boston, New
     England, & Simon Fraser, merchant in Gibralter, V.
     the children of Thomas Palmer and his wife Mary
     McIntosh in Boston, 24 Dec. 1760.   (CS16.1.107)

RUSSELL, ELIZABETH.   Elizabeth Russell, wife of Thomas
     McWilliam, farmer in New York, V. Thomas Provan,
     linen draper in Carmarthen, South Wales, 17 Jan. 1776.
                                                (CS16.1.168)

RUSSELL, MARGARET.   Margaret Russell, wife of William
     Walton, in Bristol, Pennsylvania, V. Andrew Ramsay,
     merchant in the Canongate, 16 Dec. 1773.   (CS17.1.157)

RUSSELL, MARY.   Mary Russell, & William Walton, in Bristol,
     Pennsylvania, V. Andrew Ramsay, merchant in the
     Canobgate, 6 July 1780.   (CS16.1.179)

RUTHERFORD, JOHN.   John Rutherford, surgeon in Antigua, 2nd
     son of Thomas Rutherford, merchant in Edinburgh, V.
     Andrew Rutherford, eldest son of Thomas Rutherford,
     merchant in Edinburgh, 21 Feb. 1744.   (CS16.1.73)

RUTHERFORD, ROBERT.   Robert Rutherford, merchant in
     Winchester, Virginia, Neil Snodgrass and Richard
     Templeman in Norfolk, Virginia, George Mitchell,
     assistant to Robert Rutherford, merchant in Winchester,
     Virginia, Andrew Boyd, merchant in Antigua then in
     Virginia, Patrick and Andrew Thomson in ...., & James
     Easdale, merchant in St Kitts, V. George Anderson,
     John Ingram, & John Blair, merchants in Glasgow,
     3 July 1765.   (CS16.1.122)

RYALL .... Ryall, merchant in Boston, V. the Duke
     of Gordon, 21 Nov. 1781.   (CS16.1.185)

SADDLER, JAMES.   James Saddler, merchant in St Kitts then
     in Bristol, V. Roger Hamilton McNeill of Taynish,
     27 June 1781.   (CS16.1.183)

SADDLER, WILLIAM.   William Saddler, merchant in St Kitts, V.
     Neill McNeill, merchant in Bristol then in St Kitts,
     Roger McNeill of Taynish, & James Simpson, merchant in
     Glasgow, 15 Feb. 1765.   (CS16.1.120)

SAWERS, ALEXANDER.   Alexander Sawers in Jamaica, etc, V.
     the creditors of Mungo Carrick, hosier in Edinburgh,
     20 Jan. 1773.   (CS16.1.154)

SCOTT, ANDREW. Andrew Scott, merchant & surgeon in Maryland, & John Scott of Mallemy, his brother, V. David Baird, merchant in Edinburgh, 19 Feb. 1748. (CS16.1.80)

SCOTT, ARCHIBALD. Archibald Scott, third son of Archibald Scott of Rossie and Margaret Mill, youngest daughter of James Mill of Old Montrose, legatee of her brother Charles Mill in Georgetown, South Carolina, V. Sir Alexander Ramsay of Balmain, etc, 10 July 1777. (CS16.1.171)

SCOTT, FRANCIS. Francis Scott, merchant in Dumfries then in Virginia, V. Alexander Ferguson, Commander of the Adventure of Dumfries, 27 July 1748. (CS16.1.80)

SCOTT, FRANCIS. Francis Scott, merchant in Dumfries then in Virginia, V. Elizabeth Wright, widow of Thomas Kirkpatrick, merchant in Dumfries, 8 June 1748. (CS16.1.80)

SCOTT, JOAN. Joan Scott, daughter of George Scott and Isobel Pott, in Jamaica, V. Janet Kirkpatrick of Boreland, 10 July 1779. (CS16.1.175)

SCOTT, ROBERT. Robert Scott in Grenada, Robert Scott in Blainslee, and George Scott in Blainslee, sons of Robert Scott of Blainslee, V. John Simpson in Addington, 20 Dec. 1780. (CS16.1.181)

SCOTT, ROBERT. Robert Scott, watchmaker in Fredericksburg, Virginia, V. John Breakenridge, son of John Breakenridge, watchmaker in Portsburgh, 13 Feb. 1781. (CS16.1.183)

SCOTT, THOMAS. Dr Thomas Scott in Jamaica V. John Anderson in Strichen, 9 Feb. 1783. (CS17.1.2)

SEAMAN, ELIZABETH. Elizabeth Seaman, sister of George Seaman, deceased, merchant in Charleston, South Carolina, V. John Deas, David Deas, James Lennox, and William Lennox, merchants in Charleston, South Carolina, 27 Nov. 1776. (CS16.1.170)

SEAMAN, GEORGE. George Seaman, James and John Crockatt, merchants in Charleston, South Carolina, & Charles Crockatt, merchant in Edinburgh, V. Andrew Ross, clothier in Edinburgh, 17 July 1739. (CS16.1.69)

SEAMAN, GEORGE.   George Seaman, merchant in South
   Carolina, V. John Carmichael, merchant in Edinburgh,
   21 Dec. 1756.   (AC7.49.14)

SEAMAN, GEORGE.   George Seaman, merchant in Charleston,
   South Carolina, V. Lewis Hay, merchant in Edinburgh,
   13 Dec. 1764.   (CS16.1.120)

SEMPLE, JOHN.   John Semple, merchant in Portobacco, Maryland, & James Lawson, merchant in Glasgow, V. Thomas
   Muir, mason, & James Syme in Hamilton, 12 June 1765.
                                                (CS16.1.122)

SEMPLE, JOHN.   John Semple, merchant in Portobacco, Maryland, V. James Syme, grandson of Robert Hamilton,
   vintner in Hamilton, 16 July 1765.   (CS16.1.122)

SETON, JOHN.   John Seton in Jamaica V. Allan McDougall,
   16 Dec. 1780.   (CS16.1.181)

SETON, JOHN.   John Seton in Jamaica V. Robina Seton, wife
   of Major Peter Halkett, 19 Dec. 1781.   (CS16.1.185)

SHARP, ALEXANDER.   Alexander Sharp, merchant in Perth then
   in America, V. James Buchan, 20 Feb. 1783.   (CS17.1.2)

SHAW, ALEXANDER.   Alexander Shaw, writer in Edinburgh then
   in America, V. Joseph Williamson, clerk, 20 Dec. 1780.
                                                (CS16.1.181)

SHAW, LACHLAN.   Lieutenant Lachlan Shaw of Captain Demeris's
   Independent Company in South Carolina, V. Captain
   Walter Stewart of General Ferrill's Regiment, 22 Dec.
   1756.   (CS16.1.99)

SHAW, NORMAN.   Norman Shaw, servant to Norman McLeod of
   McLeod, in America, William Hunter, surgeon in Lanark
   then in America, & Duncan McDonald, writer in Edinburgh
   then in Jamaica, V. Alexander McDonald, 2 Mar. 1779.
                                                (CS16.1.175)

SHEDDAN, JOHN.   John Sheddan, merchant in Virginia, V.
   John Leitch in Warwick, Virginia, then in Parkhead,
   Holytown, 29 Jan. 1783.   (CS17.1.2)

71

SHEDDAN, ROBERT.   Robert Sheddan, merchant in Beith then
    in Virginia,V. Alexander Aikenhead, mariner in
    Irvine, 5 Feb. 1773.   (CS16.1.154)

HEDDAN, WILLIAM.   William Sheddan, merchant in Hobshall on
    the Rappahannock River, Virginia, and Robert Sheddan,
    merchant in Portsmouth on the James River, Virginia, V.
    William Mure of Gatehead, 21 Dec. 1774.   (CS16.1.161)

SHERRIFF, JOHN.   John Sherriff in Maryland V. Speirs,
    French & Company, merchants in Glasgow, 31 July 1779.
                                                  (CS16.1.177)

SHIELS, QUEELY.   Queely Shiels, student of physick in
    Edinburgh then in the West Indies, Queely Taylor,
    Lieutenant in the British Rangers, & Sir John Ogilvy
    of Invercarity, V. James Dewar, merchant in Edinburgh,
    12 July 1781.   (CS16.1.183)

SHORT, THOMAS.   Thomas and John Short in Virginia, & Thomas
    Short in Edinburgh, V. the British Linen Company,
    10 July 1783.   (CS17.1.2)

SIMPSON, ALEXANDER.   Alexander Simpson, merchant tailor in
    Edinburgh, V. Dr Dennis Dorsey in America, 8 Oct. 1779.
                                                     (AC7.58)

SIMPSON, ANDREW.   Andrew Simpson, wright in Nova Scotia, V.
    Robert Wilson in Penicuik, 3 Aug. 1776.   (CS16.1.170)

SIMPSON, ARCHIBALD.   Archibald Simpson, merchant in Islay
    then in America, V. Alexander Ross, 29 June 1780.
                                                  (CS16.1.179)

SIMPSON, JOHN.   John Simpson of Moyret, merchant in Glasgow
    then in New London, North America, V. Alexander and
    Daniel Campbell & Company, merchants in Glasgow, 5 July
    1769.   (CS16.1.134)

SIMPSON, JOHN.   John Simpson of Grueldykes, merchant in
    Sunberry, Georgia, nephew of Thomas Cockburn, writer
    in Edinburgh, V. Edward Tyson, 17 Feb. 1774.(CS16.1.157)

SIMPSON, JOHN.   John Simpson, merchant in Sunbury, Georgia,
    V. Walter Scott, 23 Feb. 1774.   (CS16.1.157)

SIMPSON, JOHN.   John Simpson in Georgia & Rev. John
    Johnston in Biggar V. the trustees of David Wardrop,
    merchant in Edinburgh, 22 Feb. 1775.   (CS16.1.165)

SIMPSON, WILLIAM.   William Simpson in Charleston, South
    Carolina, only son of Andrew Simpson of Pendreich, V.
    Charles Rioch, merchant in Edinburgh, 16 Dec. 1780.
                                                    (CS16.1.181)

SINCLAIR, ARCHIBALD.   Archibald Sinclair in Jamaica &
    Alexander Sinclair of Lybster V. John Sinclair of Ulbster
    & John, Earl of Breadalbane, 24 Nov. 1773. (CS16.1.154)

SINCLAIR, JAMES.   James Sinclair in Nova Scotia, only son of
    Isobel Lamont sister of Lauchlin Lamont of Achagoyle, V.
    Colonel Charles Campbell of Barbreck, 25 July 1781.
                                                    (CS16.1.184)

SINCLAIR, KENNEDY.   Kennedy Sinclair, merchant in Jamaica, V.
    John McLachlane, merchant in Glasgow, 12 Feb. 1773.
                                                    (CS16.1.154)

SINCLAIR, MARGARET.   Margaret and Janet Sinclair, sisters
    of Alexander Sinclair of Auchtergall, merchant in
    Kingston, Jamaica, V. Andrew Hamilton, 21 July 1781.
                                                    (CS16.1.184)

SINCLAIR, MARGARET.   Margaret Sinclair in Jamaica V. John
    Sinclair of Ulbster, 28 Nov. 1781.   (CS16.1.185)

SINCLAIR, ROBERT.   Robert Sinclair, merchant in London then
    in New York, V. James Wilson and Sons, merchants in
    Kilmarnock, 26 June 1776.   (CS16.1.168)

SKENE, JAMES.   James Skene, physician in Carolina, William
    Roberts, physician in South Carolina, etc, V. John
    Galt, merchant in Edinburgh, 1 Mar. 1775.   (CS16.1.165)

SMITH, ALEXANDER.   Alexander Smith in Carolina V. Isabel
    Seton, widow of James Smith merchant in Haddington,
    4 Mar. 1755.   (CS16.1.95)

SMITH, ... Smith in Carolina, eldest son of James
    Smith, eldest son of Alexander Smith, Provost of
    Haddington, V. Thomas Sinclair, writer in Edinburgh,
    4 Mar. 1755.   (CS16.1.95)

SMITH, ALEXANDER.   Alexander Smith in Carolina V. Ann
    Manners, wife of John Nicolson, baker in Haddington,
    4 July 1759.   (CS16.1.105)

SNODGRASS, NEIL.   Neil Snodgrass, merchant in Virginia,
    John Snodgrass of Cunninghamhead, etc, V. Hugh
    Snodgrass, weaver in Paisley, 2 Mar. 1762. (CS16.1.114)

SOMERVILLE, JAMES.   James Somerville, merchant in Maryland,
    V. Alexander Campbell, merchant in Glasgow,
    29 July 1769.   (CS16.1.138)

SOMERVILLE, JOHN.   John Somerville in North America, George
    Somerville, merchant in North America, & William
    Somerville of Kenmore V. Agnes Somerville, daughter of
    James Somerville of Kenmore, deceased, 18 July 1765.
                                                 (CS16.1.122)

SOMERVILLE, JOHN.   John Somerville, merchant in Maryland,
    V. John Campbell, merchant in Glasgow, 5 Mar. 1771.
                                                 (CS16.1.143)

SPALDING, JAMES.   James Spalding, merchant in Florida,
    Elizabeth and Isobel Gray, daughters of John Gray of
    Rogart, etc, V. Elizabeth, Countess of Sutherland,
    7 July 1769.   (CS16.1.138)

SPALDING, JAMES.   James Spalding, merchant in Florida or
    Carolina, V. Humphrey Bland Gardner, son of Robert
    Gardner, Commissary to H M Forces, 8 July 1769.
                                                 (CS16.1.138)

SPENCE, PETER.   Peter Spence, surgeon in Virginia,
    eldest son of Peter Spence, sailor in Linlithgow, V.
    Robert Clarke, merchant in Linlithgow, 10 Mar. 1775.
                                                 (CS16.1.165)

SPENCE, ROBERT.   Robert Spence, son of William Spence,
    tailor in Edinburgh then in North America, V. Robert
    Jamieson, bookseller in Edinburgh, 11 Feb. 1783.
                                                 (CS17.1.2)

SPENCE, WALTER.   Walter Spence, merchant in New York, Anne
    Spence, Elizabeth Spence, mother of Lawrence Spence,
    writer in Edinburgh, V. Walter Spence, 28 Feb. 1783.
                                                 (CS17.1.2)

SPREULL, ANDREW.   Andrew Spreull, merchant in Gosport,
    Virginia, per his executor Thomas McCulloch, V. John
    Hunter of Frankfield, 27 July 1780.   (CS16.1.181)

SPREULL, ANDREW.   Andrew Spreull, merchant in Virginia,
    per his executor Thomas McCulloch V. Isobel Bowie,
    widow of William Gray of Gartcraig, merchant in
    Glasgow, 8 Feb. 1782.   (CS17.1.1)

SPREULL, ISOBEL.   Isobel Spreull, niece of Andrew Spreull,
    merchant in Virginia, and her husband Peter Paterson,
    merchant in Ayr, V. Thomas McCulloch in Gosport,
    Virginia, then in Glasgow, 29 June 1779.   (CS16.1.175)

SPREULL, ISOBEL.   Isobel Spreull, niece of Andrew Spreull,
    merchant in Gosport, Virginia, and her husband Peter
    Paterson, merchant in Greenock, V. Elizabeth Bowie,
    widow of William Gray, merchant in Glasgow, 29 July
    1779.   (CS16.1.177)

STARK, HENRY.   Henry Bethune Stark, Lieutenant of the 63rd
    Regiment of Foot in America, & Lieutenant Colonel
    Henry Patton V. Robert Little, farmer in Stobs, 31 July
    1781.   (CS16.1.184)

STEDMAN, CHRISTIAN.   Christian Stedman, widow of Hugh
    Steel, shipmaster in Bo'ness then commander of a
    Philadelphia privateer, V. William Hay of Lawfield,
    Charles Addison, merchant in Bo'ness, Archibald Steel,
    farmer in Stanley then in Saltcoats, etc, 8 Feb. 1763.
                                               (CS16.1.115)

STEUART, JOHN.   Sir John Steuart of Kettleston, son of
    George Steuart, surgeon apothecary in Boston, New
    England, V. Charles Mitchell of Piteady, 21 Dec. 1752.
                                               (CS16.1.89)

STEVENS, JANET.   Janet Stevens, widow of Captain Robert
    Sinclair, merchant in New York, and hisnatural son
    John Stevens V. James Wilson & Son, merchants in
    Kilmarnock, 16 July 1777.   (CS16.1.171)

STEVENSON, ROBERT.   Robert Stevenson, shipmaster in New
    York, son of William Stevenson, wright in Irvine, V.
    Eliza Stevenson in Lȯndon, daughter of William
    Stevenson, baillie of Irvine, 21 Feb. 1744. (CS16.1.75)

STEVENSON, ROBERT.   Robert and Simon Stevenson, sons of
    Robert Stevenson, shipmaster in New York, V. Jean
    Stevenson, widow of ... Ronald, merchant in Ayr, &
    sister of Elizabeth Stevenson in London, 9 July 1754.
                                               (CS16.1.92)

STEWART, ALLAN.   Allan Stewart, commander of an Independent
    Company in America, V. Alexander Ogilvie, merchant in
    Leith, 27 July 1780.   (CS16.1.181)

STEWART, ANTHONY.   Anthony Stewart, merchant in Annapolis,
    Maryland, V. Alexander Allan, merchant in Edinburgh,
    6 Mar. 1783.   (CS17.1.2)

STEWART, ARCHIBALD.   Archibald Stewart of Orchell in
    America V. David Gregorie, merchant in Dunkirk, 4 Mar.
    1778.   (CS16.1.173)

STEWART, DONALD.   Donald and Margaret Stewart, children of
    Donald Stewart, surgeon in St Dominica, V. Elizabeth
    Stewart of Glenbuckie and her husband David Stewart,
    23 Feb. 1782.   (CS17.1.1)

STEWART, HUGH.   Hugh Stewart, weaver in Glasgow then in
    America, V. James Finlay, edge tool maker in Dublin,
    1 Dec. 1779.   (CS16.1.177)

STEWART, JAMES.   James Stewart in St Thomas, Jamaica, &
    Thomas Murray, master of the Walmington V. William
    Wemyss, writer in Edinburgh, 30 Mar. 1756. (AC7.48.595)

STEWART, KATHERINE.   Katherine Stewart, spouse of Neil
    Stewart in Bridge of Tilt then in America, V. James
    Robertson of Lude, 5 Mar. 1782.   (CS17.1.1)

STEWART, NEIL.   Neil Stewart in Bridge of Tilt then in
    America, V. Donald McDougall of Caundershall, 2 Aug.
    1782.   (CS17.1.1)

STEWART, NEIL.   Neil Stewart in America V. James Robertson,
    19 Feb. 1783.   (CS17.1.2)

STEWART, PETER.   Peter Stewart, merchant in Campbelltown
    then in St Johns, V. Hector McEachan, shipmaster in
    Campbelltown, 7 Feb. 1778.   (CS16.1.173)

STEWART, ROBERT.   Robert Stewart, merchant in Campbelltown
    then in St John's Island, North America, son of James
    Stewart, excise officer in Rothesay, V. John, Earl of
    Bute, 5 Aug. 1777.   (CS16.1.171)

STEWART, ROBERT. Robert Stewart, shipmaster of the
Tynecastle, V. John Vissary, shipmaster of the
Charlotte of Philadelphia, 27 Aug. 1779.   (AC7.57)

STEWART, WILLIAM. William Stewart, merchant in Ayr then in
Jamaica, V. Agnes Stewart, wife of Alexander McCutcheon
in Woodston, 11 Mar. 1779.   (CS16.1.175)

STRATFORD, DANIEL. Daniel Stratford, merchant in New York, V.
James Henderson of Gordie, 28 Feb. 1750.   (CS16.1.84)

STURROCK, BARBARA. Barbara Sturrock, sister of James Sturrock,
in Vere, Jamaica, & Alexander Farquhar at Milk River,
Jamaica, V. Barbara Sturrock, 8 July 1777.   (CS16.1.171)

SUTHERLAND, ROBERT. Robert Sutherland in Dunrobin, Jamaica,
& John Sutherland of Pronsie V. Robert Gray of Creich,
12 July 1775.   (CS16.1.165)

SUTHERLAND, ROBERT. Robert Sutherland in Jamaica then in
Uppat, Sutherland, V. Alexander Baillie, 22 Feb. 1783.
                                             (CS17.1.2)

SUTHERLAND, WILLIAM. William Sutherland, writer in Edinburgh
then in Jamaica, V. Margaret Sutherland in Birsay,
Orkney, 1 Aug. 1783.   (CS17.1.2)

SUTHERLAND & GRANT. Sutherland & Grant, merchants in
Montreal, & James Laing, merchant in Montreal V.
Cuthbertson & Syme, merchants in Glasgow, 2 July 1783.
                                             (CS17.1.2)

SWAN, JAMES. James Swan, merchant in Boston, New England,
V. John Blackwood of Solsgirth, 2 Dec. 1778.(CS16.1.174)

SWAN, ROBERT. Robert Swan, merchant in Annapolis, Maryland,
and James McLaughlan & John Drummond, merchants in
Virginia, V. James Buchanan & David Cochrtane,
merchants in Glasgow, 19 July 1753.   (CS16.1.89)

SWAN, ROBERT. Robert Swan, merchant in Annapolis, Maryland,
V. James Johnston, merchant in Glasgow, 4 Mar. 1760.
                                            (CS16.1.107)

SWAN, ROBERT. Robert Swan, merchant in Annapolis, Maryland,
V. John Drummond & James McLauchlan, merchants in
Cecil County, Maryland, etc, 18 Jan. 1763. (CS16.1.115)

SYME, JAMES.   James Syme, merchant in Massachusetts then
     in Westminster, V. Nathaniel Wheelwright, merchant
     in Boston, 22 Jan. 1766.   (CS16.1.125)

SYME, JOHN.   John Syme, merchant in Boston, Massachusetts,
     then in Westminster, V. Colonel Simon Fraser, eldest
     son of Simon, Lord Fraser, & David Baillie, son of
     William Baillie of Rosehall, 1 Aug. 1766.   (CS16.1.126)

TAIT, WILLIAM.   William Tait, shipscarpenter on the Molly
     of Glasgow, V. John Douglas, shipmaster of the Molly
     of Glasgow, re a voyage to St Kitts, 7 Apr. 1761.
                                                 (AC7.50)

TARBET, HUGH.   Hugh Tarbet, merchant in Boston, V. George
     Brown, merchant in Glasgow, 9 Mar. 1768.   (CS16.1.133)

TAYLOR, ABRAHAM.   Abraham Taylor, shipmaster in Aberdeen
     then a shipschandler in Boston, New England, V. John
     Tower, merchant in Aberdeen, 19 Dec. 1753. (CS16.1.92)

TAYLOR, ALEXANDER.   Alexander Taylor, shipmaster of the
     Tarleton of Greenock, V. George Buchanan, shipmaster
     of the Tom Lee of Baltimore, 24 Apr. 1781. (AC7.58)

TAYLOR, JEAN.   Jean Taylor, wife of Robert Rannie,
     merchant in Jamaica then in Montrose, V. Robert
     Taylor of Borrowfield, 13 Dec. 1780.   (CS16.1.181)

TELFER, JAMES.   James Telfer in Jamaica, etc, V. William
     Glen, merchant in Glasgow, 11 Mar. 1779.   (CS16.1.175)

TENNANT, ISABEL.   Isabel Tennant, daughter of James Tennant,
     tobacconist in Glasgow, wife of Dr William Spence, in
     Glasgow then in America, V. Ann Park, 19 Feb. 1782.
                                                 (CS17.1.1)

TENNANT, JOHN.   John Tennant, merchant in St Kitts, V.
     Peter Paterson, writer in Glasgow, 19 July 1765.(AC7.51)

THIBOU, ISAAC.   Isaac Thibou in Antigua & James Howison,
     barber in Antigua, V. William Laing, maltman in Glasgow,
     6 Mar. 1783.   (CS17.1.2)

THIBOU, WALTER.   Walter Thibou in Antigua V. Janet Forbes,
     daughter of Thomas Forbes of Waterton, 15 Jan. 1772.
                                                 (CS16.1.151)

THOMSON, ADAM.   Adam Thomson, physician in Pennsylvania, V.
James Burgh, merchant in London, & Thomas and Adam
Fairholme, merchants in Edinburgh, 4 July 1744.
(CS16.1.75)

THOMSON, ADAM.   Adam Thomson, physician in Annapolis,
Maryland, V. Andrew Thomson, merchant in Edinburgh,
15 Jan. 1745.   (CS16.1.75)

THOMSON, ADAM.   Dr Adam Thomson, physician in Maryland, V.
James Summers, writer in Edinburgh, 24 Jan. 1772.
(CS16.1.148)

THOMSON, ANDREW.   Andrew Thomson, merchant in Glasgow, V.
William Snodgrass, merchant in Glasgow then in North
America, 21 June 1782.   (AC7.58)

THOMSON, CHARLES.   Charles Thomson in North America V. John
and Robert Gordon, writers in Dumfries, 6 July 1778.
(CS16.1.174)

THOMSON, JAMES.   James Thomson jr in Aberdeen then in
Jamaica V. David Morice, advocate in Aberdeen, 4 Dec.
1782.   (CS17.1.1)

THOMSON, JOHN.   John Thomson, tenant farmer in Yestermains
then in New York, V. Robert Simson, herd to George
Thomson, tenant farmer in Cliftoncot, 4 Mar. 1772.
(CS16.1.148)

THOMSON, JOHN.   John Thomson, merchant in Jamaica, &
Thomas Whitelaw, merchant in Jamaica then in Glasgow,
V. William Thomson, shipmaster in Port Glasgow,
23 Feb. 1779.   (CS16.1.175)

THOMSON, JOHN.   John Thomson in Jamaica & William Whitelaw
in Jamaica then in Glasgow V. James Haig, merchant in
Edinburgh, & Robert McKenzie in Charleston, South
Carolina, 8 Feb. 1782.   (CS17.1.2)

THOMSON, PATRICK.   Patrick Thomson, merchant in New York, V.
John Robertson, goldsmith in Edinburgh, 27 Jan. 1768.
(CS16.1.133)

THOMSON, PATRICK.   Patrick Thomson and Andrew Thomson,
merchants in Edinburgh then in New York, V. John Glen of
Assloas, merchant in Glasgow then in Kilmarnock, 25 Jan.
1769.   (CS16.1.134)

THOMSON, PATRICK.   Patrick Thomson, merchant in Hartford,
North America, V. Anderson & Dalzeill, merchants in
Glasgow, 7 Feb. 1772.   (CS16.1.148)

TOD, GEORGE.   George Tod, surgeon in Caroline County,
Virginia, eldest son of Charles Tod, merchant in West-
shore, Holme parish, Orkney, V. Patrick Graeme of
Graemeshall, 20 July 1764.   (CS16.1.117)

TOD, GEORGE.   George Tod, merchant, and William Tod, coach-
builder in Philadelphia, V. Agnes, Jean, & Stewart
Hutchison, children of William Hutchison and Agnes
Lightbody, daughter of James Lightbody, wigmaker in
Edinburgh, 9 Aug. 1782.   (CS17.1.1)

TOD, MARGARET.   Margaret Tod or Grier, widow of William
Lang, bookseller in Boston, James Lang, coppersmith in
Glasgow, & William Lang, only son of the said William
Lang, V. William Marshall, bookseller in Glasgow,
10 July 1765.   (CS16.1.122)

TOD, OLIVER.   Oliver Tod, merchant in Kingston, Jamaica, V.
Archibald Tod of Hayfield, 11 May 1762.   (AC7.50)

TOWER, ELIZABETH.   Elizabeth Tower, wife of James
Abernethy, shipscarpenter in Jamaica, etc, V. Rev. George
Cheyne in Stirling, 16 July 1779.   (CS16.1.175)

TRAILL, ROBERT.   Robert Traill, customs controller in
Portsmouth, New England, & William and John Traill, sons
of William Traill, eldest son of William Traill,
merchant in Kirkwall, V. John Traill of Westness,
26 Feb. 1772.   (CS16.1.148)

TRAN, HUGH.   Hugh Tran, merchant in St Kitts and Dominica,
V. William Miller the younger of Glenlee, 23 Jan. 1782.
                                         (CS17.1.1)

TRAN, HUGH.   Hugh Tran, merchant in St Kitts and Dominica,
V. Rev. Patrick Maxwell in Newmonkland, 23 Jan. 1782.
                                         (CS17.1.1)

TRAN, HUGH.   Hugh Tran, merchant in St Kitts and Dominica, &
John Mitchell, merchant in Virginia, V. William Miller
of Glenlee, 11 July 1783.   (CS17.1.2)

TRENT, ... Trent, son of James Trent, son of William
Trent, merchant in Pennsylvania, V. Robert Aillie,
merchant in Inverness, 14 Dec. 1757.   (CS16.1.100)

TURNBULL, CHARLES.   Charles Turnbull & Company in Dinwiddie
County, Virginia, & Robert Turnbull, merchant, V.
Simon Brown & Company, merchants in Glasgow, 8 July 1775.
(CS16.1.165)

TURNBULL, ELIZABETH.   Elizabeth Turnbull in Edinburgh,
widow of George Turnbull, merchant in Glasgow then in
Dinwiddie County, Virginia, and their sons Charles and
.... Turnbull, merchants in Virginia, V. David Turner
in Dalkeith, 26 Feb. 1777.   (CS16.1.170)

TURNBULL, THOMAS.   Thomas Turnbull in Torrery then in
America V. Major Thomas Goldie, 5 Feb. 1783. (CS17.1.2)

TURNER, ... Turner, silversmith in Jamaica, husband
of Jean Campbell, sister of James Campbell, goldsmith
in Edinburgh, V. David Spens, 7 Aug. 1773.   (CS16.1.149)

TURNER, WILLIAM.   William Turner, sailor in North Carolina,
eldest son of John Turner of Ardwall, V. John Coltart,
writer in Dumfries, 31 Jan. 1765.   (CS16.1.120)

TYNG, WILLIAM.   William Tyng, merchant in Falmouth, New
Brunswick, & John Duguid, merchant in Glasgow, V. David
Mitchell, Alexander Oliphant & Company, merchants in
Ayr, 13 June 1782.   (CS17.1.1)

URQUHART, LEONARD.   Leonard Urquhart and his son William
Urquhart in Jamaica V. Sir John Gordon of Invergordon,
25 July 1781.   (CS16.1.184)

URQUHART, WILLIAM.   William Urquhart, merchant in Tain then
in New York, V. Hugh Lennox, merchant in Dunblane,
4 Dec. 1782.   (CS17.1.1)

VAIR, JANET.   Janet Vair, widow of George Vair, in South
Carolina then in Edinburgh, V. Margaret Vair, daughter
of Janet and George Vair, in South Carolina then in
Edinburgh, William Vair, perukemaker in Edinburgh, &
Robert Syme, her tutors, 4 July 1776.   (CS16.1.168)

VAUSS, HUGH.   Hugh Vauss in Boston, New England, V. Archibald
Yuill and James Hamilton, merchants in Port Glasgow,
9 Apr. 1734.   (AC7.40.86)

VAUSS, HUGH.   Hugh Vauss, merchant in Boston, eldest son of
    John Vauss, merchant in Ayr, V. Barbara McDowall, widow
    of Colonel Patrick Vauss of Barnbarroch, 26 July 1743.
                                                (CS16.1.72)

WALKER, ALEXANDER.   Alexander Walker, merchant in Virginia,
    eldest son of Emanuel Walker, customs collector in Port
    Glasgow, V. Robert Montgomery, mariner in Larne, owner
    of the Margaret of Larne, 27 Jan. 1750.   (CS16.1.84)

WALKER, ALEXANDER.   Alexander Walker, merchant & factor in
    Virginia, eldest son of Emanuel Walker, customs
    collector in Port Glasgow, V. Alexander Drummond,
    customs collector in Greenock, Nov. 1749.   (SC16.1.81)

WALKER, ALEXANDER.   Alexander Walker, merchant & Factor in
    Virginia, & Daniel Campbell of Shawfield V. Alexander
    Drummond, customs collector in Greenock, 11 Jan. 1751.
                                                (CS16.1.85)

WALKER, EMANUEL.   Emanuel Walker in New York, only son of
    Alexander Walker, merchant in Port Glasgow, John
    Mitchell, merchant in Virginia, James Denny in America,
    son of James Denny, schoolmaster in Greenock, etc, V.
    Hugh Tran, merchant in St Kitts and Dominica, 3 Feb.
    1779.   (CS16.1.174)

WALKER, EMANUEL.   Emanuel Walker in New York, son of
    Alexander Walker of Craigbate, V. John McKerrol,
    merchant in Maxwelltown, 18 Dec. 1782.   (CS17.1.1)

WALKER, JAMES.   James Walker, surgeon in Jamaica, V. Gavin
    Walker, miller at Newmill of Kilmarnock, 2 July 1783.
                                                (CS17.1.2)

WALKER, WILLIAM.   William Walker in Antigua then in
    St Vincent, James Warden, merchant in St Croix, &
    Edward Jones of Esdaile & Jones, merchant in Basseterre,
    St Kitts, V. Robert Allason, merchant in Glasgow,
    1 July 1778.   (CS16.1.173)

WALLACE, MARGARET.   Margaret Wallace, widow of John Kinnear,
    merchant in Kingston, Jamaica, V. John Wallace, merchant
    in Glasgow, 13 July 1781.   (CS16.1.183)

WALLACE, MARY.   Mary Wallace, widow of John Kinnear,
    merchant in Kingston, Jamaica, V. William Wallace jr,
    merchant in Glasgow, 12 Dec. 1781.   (CS16.1.184)

WANDS, GEORGE.   George Wands in Jamaica then in Hamilton V.
James Gardner, mason in England, 4 July 1781.(CS16.1.183)

WARDEN, HUGH.   Hugh Warden, merchant in Perth then in
Virginia, V. David Thom, merchant in Dundee, 10 Mar. 1774.
(CS16.1.157)

WARDROP, JAMES.   James Wardrop, merchant in Maryland, V.
John Buchanan, merchant in London, 8 Dec. 1761.
(CS16.1.110)

WARDROP, WILLIAM.   William Wardrop, merchant in St Kitts, &
James Grieve, tobacconist in London, V. William Cheap,
linen manufacturer in Edinburgh, 16 Feb. 1774.(CS16.1.157)

WATSON, GILBERT.   Gilbert Watson, mason in Kirkintilloch
then in America, V. James Denniston, eldest son of James
Denniston, tenant farmer in Balgrochan, 2 Feb. 1776.
(CS16.1.168)

WATSON, JOHN.   John Watson, merchant in South Carolina, &
George Richardson, writer in Edinburgh, V. Thomas
Bailliie in Charleston, 22 Nov. 1743.   (CS16.1.72)

WATSON, JOHN.   John Watson, John Crockat, Kenneth McLie and
William Woodrop, merchants in Charleston, South
Carolina, V. Thomas Baillie, merchant in Charleston,
South Carolina, 22 Feb. 1745.   (CS16.1.78)

WATSON, WILLIAM.   William James Watson in South Carolina,
son of John Watson in North Carolina, V. John Warrand,
merchant in Glasgow, 25 Nov. 1772.   (CS16.1.151)

WEDDERBURN, JAMES.   Dr James Wedderburn in Jamaica then in
Inveresk V. Helen Halkerston, 2 Dec. 1780. (CS16.1.181)

WEDDERSTON, JOHN.   John Wedderston, youngest son of John
Wedderston smith, surgeon in Kingston, Jamaica, V.
Marion Wedderston, wife of John Currer, butcher in
Galashiels, 20 July 1773.   (CS16.1.157)

WEEKS, THOMAS.   Thomas Pyme Weeks, son of William Burt Weeks,
in Nevis, V. William Gordon, 16 Dec. 1772. (CS16.1.151)

WEIR, ROBERT. Robert Weir in Unity Estate, Portland,
Jamaica, & William Weir, youngest son of Robert Weir
of Symington, V. Sibbala McCoul, widow of Ralf Weir
in Moss-side, 2 July 1778.   (CS16.1.173)

WELSH, JOHN. John Welsh, merchant in Leith then in Jamaica,
V. Archibald McLarty, shipmaster in Greenock, 11 Apr.
1769.   (AC7.53)

WHEELWRIGHT, NATHANIEL. Nathaniel Wheelwright, merchant
in New England, & Colonel Simon Fraser, eldest son of
Simon, Lord Fraser, V. John Syme, merchant in
Westminster, 10 July 1766.   (CS16.1.125)

WHITE, HUGH. Hugh White, merchant in Glasgow then in
Boston, etc, V. John Auchincloss, merchant in Glasgow,
& John Paisley, merchant in Paisley, 4 Dec. 1766.
                                               (CS16.1.126)

WHITE, HUGH. Hugh White, merchant in Glasgow then in
Crown Point, North America, V. Thomas Kerr & Company,
merchants in Paisley, 4 Aug. 1778.   (CS16.1.174)

WHITE, JAMES. James White of Waterside in Carbolton,
St Thomas-in-the-East, Jamaica, V. John White, tenant
farmer in Waterside, 16 June 1781.   (CS16.1.183)

WHITE, JOHN. John White in Frederick County, Virginia, V.
the Clerks of Session, 15 Feb. 1766.   (CS16.1.125)

WHITE, JOHN. John White, merchant in Philadelphia, V.
Edward Maxwell of Straquhan, 22 Jan. 1768. (CS16.1.133)

WHYTE, HENRY. Henry Whyte, merchant and sailor in Boston,
V. Andrew Johnston sr, merchant in Anstruther, 14 Dec.
1763.   (CS16.1.117)

WIGHTMAN, CHARLES. Charles Wightman, merchant in Tobago,
son of Charles Wightman, merchant in Anstruther, V. the
Earl of Kelly, 11 Aug. 1778.   (CS16.1.174)

WILKIE, JOHN. John Wilkie, cooper in Charleston, South
Carolina, & James Glen, son of James Glen, in London, V.
Janet Lorimer, widow of James Glen in Blackton, 14 July
1769.   (CS16.1.138)

WILLIAMS & TOD.   Williams & Tod, merchants in Philadelphia,
    V. Robert Clarke in Linlithgow, 15 July 1778.(CS16.1.173)

WILLIAMSON, JAMES.   James Williamson, tailor in Glasgow then
    in America, V. William Gardner, weaver in Glasgow,
    16 July 1783.   (CS17.1.2)

WILLIAMSON, PETER.   Peter Williamson in Pennsylvania then
    in Aboyne, Aberdeenshire, son of James Williamson in
    Kirnley, V. Alexander Cushnie, Alexander Robertson, and
    the magistrates and merchants of Aberdeen, 26 June 1759.
                                              (CS16.1.105)

WILLIAMSON, ROBERT.   Robert Williamson in Sheriffbrae, Leith,
    then in Jamaica, etc, V. William Anderson, 16 Dec. 1778.
                                              (CS16.1.174)

WILLIAMSON, WALTER.   Walter Williamson, surgeon in Maryland,
    son of Walter Williamson of Chappleton, Dunbartonshire,
    V. Robert Mitchell, merchant in Dunbarton, 4 Aug. 1756.
                                               (CS16.1.99)

WILLS, ROBERT.   Robert Wills, merchant in Charleston, South
    Carolina, Archibald Ingram, merchant in Glasgow, McNeil
    & Claxton, merchants in St Kitts, etc, V. William
    Crawford & Company, merchants in Glasgow, & George
    Carmichael & Company, merchants in Glasgow, 16 Feb. 1758.
                                              (CS16.1.100)

WILLS, ROBERT.   Robert Wills, bookseller in Charleston,
    South Carolina, & John Spence, surgeon in Kinghorn, V.
    William Coke, bookseller in Leith, 2 Feb. 1774.
                                              (CS16.1.157)

WILSON, ALEXANDER.   Alexander Wilson of Shielhall in St Kitts
    V. William Bertram of Nisbet, 9 Dec. 1777. (CS16.1.171)

WILSON, ALEXANDER.   Alexander Wilson in St Kitts V. Thomas
    Wilson of Southfield, schoolmaster in Crawford, 9 Dec.
    1777.   (CS16.1.171)

WILSON, ALEXANDER.   Alexander Wilson of Shielhall in St Kitts
    V. Andrew Carmichael, writer in Edinburgh, 9 Dec. 1777.
                                              (CS16.1.171)

WILSON, DAVID.   David Wilson, carpenter in Greenock then in
    America, V.Robert Alexander, merchant in Glasgow,
    4 Dec. 1782.   (CS17.1.1)

WILSON, JANET. Janet and Jacobina Wilson, daughters of John
Wilson, shipmaster in Ayr then a merchant in Nansedmond,
Virginia, & Thomas Norflect, tobacco inspector in
Nansedmond, Virginia, husband of said Janet Wilson, &
Pate Wills Milner, planter in Butt County, North
Carolina, husband of said Jacobina Wilson, V. William
Gardner of Ladykirk, writer in Ayr, 7 Mar. 1776.
(CS16.1.168)

WILSON, PHILIP. Philip Wilson, planter in St Kitts, V.
Dr James Douglas of Cavers, 16 June 1778. (CS16.1.173)

WILSON, PHILIP. Philip Wilson, planter in St Kitts, son of
William Wilson of Soonhope, V. Robert Wilson, coachmaker
in Edinburgh, and his wife Mary Brown, 15 Feb. 1780.
(CS16.1.179)

WILSON, PHILIP. Philip Wilson, planter in St Kitts, eldest
son of William Wilson of Soonhope, V. Thomas Wilson in
Tobago, son of said William Wilson, 6 July 1781.
(CS16.1.183)

WILSON, PHILIP. Philip Wilson, planter in St Kitts, eldest
son of William Wilson of Soonhope, writer in Edinburgh,
V. William Simpson, feuar in Gordonlee, 19 July 1781.
(CS16.1.184)

WILSON, PHILIP. Philip Wilson, planter in St Kitts, eldest
son of William Wilson of Soonhope, & John Hamilton in
Tobago V. Sir John Whitefoord of Whitefoord, 5 Mar. 1782.
(CS17.1.1)

WILSON, PHILIP. Philip Wilson, merchant in St Kitts, V.
James Home Rigg of Morton, 7 Aug. 1783. (CS17.1.2)

WILSON, THOMAS. Thomas Wilson in Pennsylvania V. Mark Stark,
merchant in Dunfermline, 20 Feb. 1773. (CS16.1.154)

WITHERSPOON, JOHN. John Witherspoon, President of the
College of New Jersey, V. Robert Hunter, merchant in
Paisley, 30 June 1775. (CS16.1.165)

WITHERSPOON, JOHN. Dr John Witherspoon, President of the
College of New Jersey, William Houston, maltster in
Renfrew, and other members of the Scots America Company,
V. Archibald Paisley, 17 July 1779. (CS16.1.175)

WODDROP, THOMAS.   Thomas Woddrop, shipmaster in Virginia,
    V. his brother John Woddrop, son of Thomas Woddrop,
    maltman in Glasgow, 11 July 1765.   (CS16.1.122)

WOOD, JOHN.   Captain John Wood, of the Jenny of Greenock then
    in America, V. Parker, Hunter & Smith, merchants in
    Kilmarnock, 1 Dec. 1773.   (CS16.1.157)

WOOD, JOHN.   John Wood, shipmaster of the Cato in North
    America, V. John Brown, merchant in Glasgow, 1 Mar. 1774.
                                               (CS16.1.157)

WRIGHT, GEORGE.   George Wright in New York V. James Gammel
    of Park, merchant in Greenock, 17 June 1783. (CS17.1.2)

WRIGHT, ISOBEL.   Isobel Wright, wife of James Henderson in
    St Vincent, V. Robert Lawrie, accountant in Edinburgh,
    16 Feb. 1782.   (CS17.1.1)

WRIGHT, JERMYN.   Jermyn Wright, merchant in South Carolina
    then in London, V. James Steill in Bolton Ford, brother
    of Robert Steill of Bowhouses, 26 Feb. 1755. (CS16.1.95)

WRIGHT, JERMYN.   Jermyn Wright, Charles Wright, & John Home,
    in Charleston, South Carolina, V. Robert Deas, son of
    David Deas, shipmaster in Leith, 15 July 1755.(CS16.1.95)

WRIGHT, ROBERT.   Robert Wright, surgeon of the Alexander in
    Virginia, V. John Murray, druggist in Edinburgh,
    14 Jan. 1761.   (CS16.1.107)

YATER, JOSEPH.   Joseph Yater, merchant in Virginia, John
    Mitchell, merchant in Fraserburgh, Vrginia, Daniel
    Baxter, bookseller in Glasgow, etc, V. George McCall,
    merchant in Glasgow, 8 July 1775.   (CS16.1.165)

YOOL, JOHN.   John Yool, merchant in Paisley then in Boston,
    New England, V. William Wilson, 8 Aug. 1778.(CS16.1.174)

YOUNG, CHARLES.   Charles Young, son of James Young in
    Kirriemuir then in America, V. Alexander Thom, merchant
    in Dundee, 28 June 1780.   (CS16.1.179)

YOUNG, JAMES.   James Young, tailor in Falkirk then in
    America, and his wife Christian Walker V. William
    Young, tailor in Falkirk, his father, 3 Mar. 1781.
                                                (CS16.1.183)

YOUNG, JAMES.   James Young of Netherfield, merchant in
    North Carolina, and his wife Lilias Alston V.
    Alexander Elmsly in North Carolina then in London,
    23 Feb. 1781.   (CS16.1.183)

YOUNG, JOHN.   John Young, saddler & ironmonger in New York,
    & Alexander Finny, wright in Portsburgh, V. William
    Young, writer in Edinburgh,3 July 1776.   (CS16.1.168)

YOUNG, WILLIAM.   William Young, cooper in Paisley then in
    Christianbridge, Philadelphia, V. James Young, son of
    John Young in Boddam, schoolmaster in Beith, & John
    Gardner, workman in Beith, son of William Gardner,
    tenant farmer in Bogston, 30 June 1773.   (CS16.1.154)

YULE, ANDREW.   Andrew Yule, tailor in Kingston, Jamaica, V.
    Thomas Anderson, brother, and Agnes & Lillias Anderson,
    sisters of Robert Anderson, surgeon in Newmill of Ayr
    then in Kingston, Jamaica, 9 July 1782.   (CS17.1.1)

YUILL, JAMES.   James Yuill, merchant in Boston, and his
    father Claud Yuill in Strathaven V. James Cochran of
    Brownside, 10 Aug. 1763.   (CS16.1.115)

YUILL, JOHN.   John Yuill in Glasgow then in Boston, son of
    Alexander Yuill, merchant in Boston, V. Robert Crawford
    & Company, merchants in Glasgow, 15 Feb. 1781.(CS16.1.183)

INDEX TO SHIPS

INDEX TO COLONISTS

```
Borthwick John                       6
Boswell David                        6
Bowie William                       49
Boyd Andrew                         69
Boyd James                        7, 8
Boyd John                            7
Boyd Mary                            7
Boyd Robert                          7
Boyd Spencer                         7
Boyle Agnes                          8
Boyle James                       7, 8
Boyle John                        7, 8
Breadie Robert                       8
Brisbane Edward                      8
Brown George                         8
Brown, Grierson & Co                 8
Brown Gustavus                       8
Brown Thomas                         8
Brown William                        8
Brown ......                         9
Bruce Betty                          9
Bruce James                          9
Bryce Alexander                      9
Bryce Robert                        15
Buchanan Andrew                      9
Buchanan Archibald                   9
Buchanan George                 10, 78
Buchanan John                       43
Buchanan Neil                       10
Buchanan William                    10
Buntein Thomas                      10
Burd James                          10
Burke Tobias                        10
Burn Finley                         10
Burn James                          10
Burn John                           10
Burn Mary                           10
Burton William                      11
Cameron Richard                     11
Campbell Alexander                1, 11
Campbell Angus                      11
Campbell Archibald               11, 12
Campbell Charles                    12
Campbell Colin                   12, 13
Campbell Donald                     12
Campbell Dougall                    12
Campbell Duncan                     12
Campbell Gilbert                    12
Campbell James                      12
Campbell Jean                       81
Campbell John                    12, 13
Campbell Magdalene                  13
Campbell Mungo                      13
Campbell Peter                      33
Campbell Robert                     12
Campbell William                 12, 13
Campbell, Blane & Co                14
Carruthers James                    14
Carruthers Robert                   14
Chalmers Donald                     14
Chalmers James                      14
Chalmers Ronald                     14
Chapman Daniel                      14
```

```
Chew Joseph                                      38
Chisholm William                         14,  59
Christie Adam                                    14
Christie Robert                                  14
Clark Alexander                                  15
Clark Daniel                                     15
Clark George                                     15
Clark Thomas                                     15
Clark ....                                       15
Clarkson Thomas                                  15
Cleghorn Thomas                                  45
Clitheroe ....                                   13
Cochran David                        15,  28,  62
Cochran Richard                                  16
Cochran William                          16,  36
Cogle Richard                                    58
Cole George                                      16
Colquhoun Walter                                 16
Cook John                                        16
Copland William                                  16
Corbet Joseph                                    32
Corrie Archibald                                 16
Corrie Joseph                                    16
Corrie Walter                                    16
Craig John                                       17
Craigdallie Hugh                                 17
Craigdallie Janet                                17
Cramond John                             14,  17
Crawford David                                   17
Crawford George                                  17
Crawford Janet                                   17
Crichton John                                    64
Crockatt James                      17,  67,  70
Crockatt John              17,  18,  67,  70,  83
Cross David                                      18
Cumming Robert                                   18
Cumming Thomas                                   51
Cunningham Alexander                             15
Cunningham Daniel                                18
Cunningham George                                18
Cunningham Henry                                 18
Cunningham Robert                                18
Cunningham William                               18
Currie David                                     18
Currie Robert                                    18
Currie Walter                                    18
Cuthbert George                                  19
Cuthbert James                                   19
Cuthbert Joseph                                  19
Cuthbert Lewis                           19,  62
Dallas Ann                                       19
Dallas Clere                                     19
Dallas Elizabeth                                 19
Dallas Katherine                                 19
Dallas Nathan                                    19
Dallas Rachel                                    19
Dallas Robert                                    19
Dalrymple Walter                                 19
Dalrymple David                                  19
Danskine James                                   19
```

```
Deans Jean                                  20
Deas David                             20, 70
Deas John                              20, 70
Demeris ....                                71
Denny James                            20, 82
Dewar Margaret                              20
Dewar Robert                                20
Dick William                                20
Dickson John                                20
Dickson William                             20
Doig Anne                                   21
Doig William                                21
Donald Robert                          21, 50
Donaldson James                         4, 21
Donaldson William                           21
Dorsey Dennis                               72
Douglas Alexander                           21
Douglas Archibald                           21
Drew Robert                                 21
Drummond John              21, 22, 56, 77
Drummond Robert                             22
Duff William                                22
Dun James                                   22
Dunbar Charles                              22
Dunbar George                               22
Dunbar Grace                                22
Dunbar James                                22
Dunbar John                                 22
Dunbar William                              68
Duncan Alexander                            22
Duncan Andrew                      22, 23, 24
Duncan Charles                              23
Duncan Charles Erskine                      23
Duncan David                                23
Duncan John                        22, 23, 24
Duncan Margaret                             23
Duncan Thomas                      22, 23, 24
Duncan William                10, 22, 23, 24
Dunlop Archibald                            24
Dunlop James                           24, 25
Dunlop & Ralston                            25
Easdale James                               69
Edgar James                            26, 45
Edmonstone William                          26
Elliot John                                 26
Elmsley Alexander                      26, 88
Erskine John                                26
Esdaile & Jones                             82
Eustace Hancock                             26
Eustace John                                26
Fairholm Thomas                             27
Fairley James                               27
Falconer William                            27
Farquhar Alexander                          77
Farquhar Thomas                             32
Farquharson Margaret                        65
Ferguson Hugh                               27
Ferguson Robert                             27
```

```
Leall John                            42
Learmonth Alexander                   42
Learmonth John                        42
Leigh Amelia                          42
Leigh Austin                          42
Leitch John                           71
Leith John                            42
Leith Robert                          43
Leith Margaret                        43
Lennox James                      20, 70
Lennox William                    20, 70
Leslie Andrew                         43
Lesly Alexander                       43
Lewis Matthew                         43
Lewis William                         43
Lightfoot Philip                      63
Lightfoot William                     63
Lithgow Thomas                        43
Littlejohn William                     3
Livingstone Muscoe                    43
Loch Robert                            1
Lochhead Henry                    36, 43
Lock George                           44
Lockard Henry                         44
Logan George                          44
Logan Thomas                          44
Lord Samuel                           36
Lothian Andrew                        44
Love William                          44
Lovel John                            44
Lovel Thomas                          44
Lundie Archibald                      44
Lyle James                        36, 44
Lyle John                             10
Malcolm Dugald                        45
Malcolm William                       65
Marshall John                         45
Marshall William                      45
Mather John                       26, 45
Maxwell Matthew                       45
Mein Janet                        40, 46
Menzies John                          46
Menzies Ninian                        57
Middleton Peter                       46
Mikle John                    10, 45, 46
Mill Charles                          70
Miller David                          46
Miller George                         46
Miller Hugh                           46
Miller James                          47
Miller John                           47
Miller Robert                         47
Miller Thomas                         47
Miller William                    47, 64
Milligan David                        47
Milner Pate                           86
Mirrylees Alexander                   47
```

```
Simpson Andrew                              72
Simpson Archibald                           72
Simpson James                               17
Simpson John                             8, 72
Simpson William                             73
Simson John                                 38
Simson Matthew                              38
Sinclair Alexander                          73
Sinclair Archibald                          73
Sinclair James                              73
Sinclair Kennedy                            73
Sinclair Margaret                       52, 73
Sinclair Robert                         73, 75
Skene James                                 73
Skinner Thomas                              45
Smith ....                                  73
Smith Alexander                             73
Smith Archibald                             13
Snodgrass Neil                          69, 74
Snodgrass William                           79
Soloman Abraham                              1
Somerville George                           74
Somerville James                            74
Somerville John                             74
Spalding James                              74
Spence Peter                                74
Spence Robert                           10, 74
Spence Walter                               74
Spence William                              78
Spreull Andrew                          74, 75
Stafford George                             43
Stark Henry                                 75
Stedman Christian                           75
Steel Hugh                                  75
Steuart Charles                             55
Stevens Janet                               75
Stevens John                                75
Stevenson Robert                            75
Stevenson Simon                             75
Stewart Adam                                15
Stewart Alexander                           15
Stewart Allan                               76
Stewart Anthony                             76
Stewart Archibald                           76
Stewart Donald                              76
Stewart George                              75
Stewart Hugh                                76
Stewart James                               76
Stewart Katherine                           76
Stewart Margaret                            76
Stewart Neil                                76
Stewart Peter                               76
Stewart Robert                          51, 76
Stewart Roger                               51
Stewart William                             77
Stratford Daniel                            77
Sturrock James                              77
Sutherland Robert                           77
Sutherland William                          77
Sutherland & Grant                          77
```

```
Swan James                            77
Swan Robert                           77
Syme James                            78
Syme John                             78
Tarbet Hugh                           78
Taylor Abraham                        78
Taylor Jean                           78
Telfer James                          78
Telfer Patrick                        58
Templeman Richard                     69
Tennant Isobel                        78
Tennant John                          78
Thibou Isaac                          78
Thibou Walter                         78
Thomson Adam                          79
Thomson Andrew                    69, 79
Thomson Charles                       79
Thomson Duncan                        36
Thomson James                         79
Thomson John                  32, 55, 79
Thomson Patrick               69, 79, 80
Tod George                            80
Tod Margaret                          80
Tod Oliver                            80
Tod William                           80
Tower Elizabeth                       80
Traill Robert                         80
Tran Hugh                     47, 80, 82
Trent ....                            81
Trent James                           81
Trent William                         81
Turnbull Charles                      81
Turnbull Elizabeth                    81
Turnbull George                       81
Turnbull Thomas                       81
Turnbull & Shaw                       30
Turner ....                           81
Turner James                          32
Turner William                        81
Tyng William                          81
Urquhart Leonard                      81
Urquhart William                      81
Vair George                           81
Vair Janet                            81
Vair Margaret                         81
Vauss Hugh                        81, 82
Vissary John                          77
Walker Alexander                      82
Walker David                          15
Walker Emanuel                        82
Walker James                          82
Walker William                        82
Wallace Margaret                      82
Walton William                        69
Wands George                          83
Warden Hugh                           83
Warden James                          82
Wardrop James                         83
Wardrop William                       83
```

```
Watson Gilbert                        83
Watson John                        4, 83
Watson William                        83
Wedderburn James                      83
Wedderston John                       83
Weeks Thomas                          83
Weeks William                         83
Weir Robert                           84
Welsh John                            84
Wheelwright Nathaniel             78, 84
White Henry                           84
White Hugh                            84
White James                           84
White John                            84
Whitelaw Thomas                   55, 79
Wightman Charles                      84
Wilkie John                           84
Williams & Tod                        84
Williamson James                      85
Williamson Peter                      85
Williamson Robert                     85
Williamson Walter                     85
Williamson, Grieve & McNeill          15
Wills Robert                          85
Wilson Alexander                      85
Wilson David                          85
Wilson Jacobina                       86
Wilson Janet                          86
Wilson John                           86
Wilson Philip                         86
Wilson Robert                         30
Wilson Thomas                         86
Winter Thomas                         62
Witherspoon John                      86
Woddrop Thomas                        87
Woddrow Alexander                     58
Woodrop William                       83
Woodrow Alexander                     58
Wright George                         87
Wright Isabel                         87
Wright Jermyn                         87
Wright Robert                         87
Wrightman Charles                     13
Yater Joseph                          87
Yool John                             87
Young Charles                         87
Young James                       26, 88
Young John                        63, 88
Young William                         88
Yuill Alexander                       88
Yuill James                           88
Yuill John                            88
Yule Andrew                           88
```

www.ingramcontent.com/pod-product-compliance
Lightning Source LLC
Chambersburg PA
CBHW070840300326
41935CB00038B/1265